# Boki

*By*

## Jimmy J. Holloway

ARPress
ILLUMINATING IDEAS.
EMPOWERING VOICES

**ARPress**
45 Dan Road Suite 5
Canton MA 02021
Hotline: 1(888) 821-0229
Fax:      1(508) 545-7580

Ordering Information:
Quantity sales. Special discounts are available on quantity purchases by corporations, associations, and others. For details, contact the publisher at the address above.

Printed in the United States of America.

ISBN-13:   Paperback    979-8-89676-296-6
           Ebook        979-8-89676-297-3

Library of Congress Control Number: 2025910856

# Table of Contents

# Dedication

This book is dedicated to three strong women in my life:

My grandmother – Elease Mary Perry Holloway

My mother – Rosalyn Holloway

My aunt – Cynthia (Tuti) Holloway Green.

These are the women who inspired my soul. They nurtured and healed me when I bled, and they comforted me when I cried. They always prayed for and believed in me. They always said, "Booky, everything's going to be alright!"

To all who knew me, my heart, and my family, the struggles, tragedy, pain, and growth—through it all, there were plenty of joyous times and love. I have special fond memories of those times, people, and places. I will attempt to take you on a few of the journeys through my life. I hope you will cry, laugh, and leave with a lasting memory of an era that few have knowledge of or understand.

If my book is successful, I'd like to extend a gracious thank you to God, whose love and grace gave me the ability to write this book. I cannot forget my third-grade teacher, Mrs. Steiner, who taught me how to read and write. She always told me, "If you read the newspaper, you can have the history of tomorrow."

Grandma, Elease Mary Perry Holloway, for without her, there would be no me or book. In keeping it short and sweet: Get to reading.

# Acknowledgments

I would like to take this opportunity to acknowledge those in my life who had a great wealth of life experiences and knowledge for myself and others. No one is born with an understanding and wisdom of life. What I have now is new experiences and understanding. So, I'd like to thank you. Enjoy my book.

MY HIGHEST POWER WHO GAVE ME MY SPIRIT

GWENDOLYN ANN HOWARD for the many hours she spent assisting me in the preparation of my book.

I'd like to acknowledge a dear friend, DANA HOLIDAY, a beautiful soul who never hesitates to care for the well-being of others without a thought.

My friend, DONALD JOE, whose life I saved when he was drowning. He, in turn, saved mine. When I was attacked with a bat, he threw me a stick to defend myself. We grew up together as kings.

CURTIS VANLIEROP answered every question I'd ever asked him. Curtis had a deep understanding of many things in life, for which I am thankful. I have learned much, and I will now thank you all.

VANCE WRIGHT for his friendship, love, and the respect we had for one another. He was two days older than me, but he's no longer here. He is missed. He'd always say, "I'm right when I'm wrong!"

HORACE WILLIAMS III: Thank you for responding quickly and seeing the vision on paper and maybe one day on screen. You're giving me the opportunity to share my vision of my book.

Thank you to my editors, LILAC and ADAM GRAY.

# PIMP MAGIC

MY HAIR, MY CLOTHES, AND THE WAY I STROLL,

SMOOTH, MELLOW, ALWAYS IN CONTROL.

SEASONED GENEROUSLY WITH SOULFUL WORDS
AND MELODIES INSIDE MY MOTHER'S WOMB I
HEARD.

THE ESSENCE OF ME IS THEM THAT CAME AND
PLAYED BEFORE ME,

SOOTHING TO MY SOUL.

EASED MY SPIRIT WHENEVER I CRIED DEEP...

YOU LIFTED ME HIGHER.

# Introduction

This is a story about my life and how I grew up. My grandma, who raised me, called me the first name I've known, which is Boki, the title of this book. She taught me many things and prayed for me along with two other women: my mother, Rosalyn, and my aunt, Tutie. As the firstborn, I had a big responsibility on my shoulders and many obstacles to overcome, along with the tears and pain I endured from childhood to adulthood.

Learning life without a father, two brothers, and two sisters meant I had to change diapers back when there were no Pampers. We had to bust suds in the tub. I'm not going to make excuses for what I did, whether it was due to poverty or not having a father. My mother always said, "If you make your bed hard, you're the only one that's gonna sleep in it." These women pointed out many things that helped me become who I am today: a product of my environment.

I learned to read by reading the news at ten and eleven in 1967. I was drinking coffee and eating cornbread after listening to gospel music, and my grandma talked to me all night long. She and my aunt used to buy all these religious creams and liquids and put them in my tub and on me. After reading this story, you might understand that prayer works. I know it did for me.

New York was brimming with alcohol, dope, and cocaine—the rich man's high. Beer and wine were for those who had the least. Here in this book are keys to avoiding and saving yourselves from ever thinking this was a glorious life. It makes for great reading. Enjoy!

# Chapter One

Jimm's earliest possible recollection of himself was… me looking down on myself. Although I might have spent many days and months at this location in Brooklyn, I clearly remember playing in backyards, always alone, looking for treasures. Once, I found a white wall tire; to me, that was so cool. I played so hard with it that day, and I enjoyed playing with it so much that I brought it home to keep it for tomorrow.

The minute my mother saw it, she said, "Boy, get that dirty tire out of this house right away."

I said, "But it's a white wall tire, Mom."

"I don't care! Get it out of here," she strictly said this time.

Disappointed with my mom's decision, I moved out but hid the tire in the backyard. While there, I saw a little baby kitten. It was so cute, and I thought, *This must come home with me. Mom can't reject this cute, cuddly kitty cat.* Feeling happy, I returned home with the kitten.

Once home, I showed the litten to my mom, saying, Mommy! Look what I have found."

I guess she liked it at first, but it was a fleeting moment of happiness for me. When we turned the kitten over to see its sex, we saw a lot of fleas on its belly.

Mom exclaimed with disgust, "Augh! Get it out now!"

I was mad, but having heard that cats have nine lives, I took it up on the roof and threw it off to see if it survived. Then I ran down to see if it was true. When I picked it up, it was still alive, though barely. I started flinging it up in the air. Since no one had seen me throw it off the roof, I wasn't in trouble.

When I went to the roof, past the fifth floor, I heard music playing. I said to myself, "That's a party." Along with music, I heard kids laughing and playing, and when I knocked on the door, a woman opened it and said, "Hi."

"Hi! Can I come in? I saw party lights and food."

"Oh, no, little boy; you're too dirty; you got to wash up and put nice clothes on if you want to join the party."

Excited, I ran down four flights of stairs. The moment I entered my home, I said, "Mommy, Mommy. I wanna go to this party upstairs. The lady said I'm too dirty to join the party. Please, dress me up fast."

Mom said, "You really are at this moment. You're too light to get that dirty! Look at your arms and hands; they're black as coal."

"I need nice clothes, Mom," I almost pleaded.

Mom said, "Of course, you do. First, look at your arms." She turned my arm over. "Come on then, take your clothes off and get in this tub. There, look at that dirt. See, it shows on you more 'cause you're light skin."

Well, after her sermon and scrubbing, she dressed me, and I ran back upstairs to the fifth floor and knocked on the door. When it opened, the person said, "Sorry, little man, the party is over."

That was the greatest hurt, more than the tire or the kitten. I was feeling hurt and looking to get over some of my feelings; right next door to them was a vacant apartment, not fully vacant, though. There was a mattress; I pulled it up, dragged it to the walls next to them, and set it on fire. I can't remember if I told my mother this and the effort I took to start that fire. Well, the building burnt down. I can't remember if I got blamed or punished for that. I can't remember if I was six years old or maybe younger, but that act was very strong for my age. Well, they kicked us out of Brooklyn.

BACK TO HARLEM

112th Street, 1161 Lenox Avenue.

I would play in Central Park. One day, I wandered over to listen to the message a man was preaching on civil rights. It was for the betterment of black people, but not everyone there had the same interest. This man had a big black bag on the ground by his foot; he said, "It's medical stuff, and I'm a doctor. Would you want a bag like this one?"

"Of course, yes," I said.

"Well, follow me," he said.

He led me into an abandoned storefront with broken glass strewn around. It smelled of fire. As he reached the end of the store, he turned around, put the bag down, and began to pull things out—gauzes, cream, and bandages. He then gestured for me to come.

As I approached him, he began to wrap gauze around my head and took out some kind of cream; it must've been petroleum jelly, I think.

As he rubbed that cream on my head, he said, "Turn around and pull down your pants."

I turned around and took off running toward the door; maybe three steps away, I tripped and fell. While I was falling, something big flew over my head and crashed in front of me. Quickly, I got to my feet somehow and ran out screaming.

As I ran out of the storefront, I found my grandma. She took me in her arms, and while rocking me, she started humming gospel songs and took me home. Once upstairs, she said, "Let us pray for him, Bookie."

I could not understand that! I never asked, but I thought, "Pray for him? Grandma, let's go find him and kick his ass all the way in."

It took me many years to understand forgiveness. Time to leave Harlem.

## BURNOUT IN BROOKLYN!

Burnout in Brooklyn and almost molested in Harlem, we were headed to the Bronx, Clinton Avenue, right off Boston Road. Like Harlem, there was a park—Crotona Park. King Charles, the unicycle rider, started there. There were plenty of backyards to play in. While moving, I noticed a crib with a baby and a brother I had to protect. My first fight was for him, with Alan Smith. It was strange back then; you fought and shook hands afterward—best of friends for some and not so much for others.

I found out that I had an uncle, John Scott Holloway—young, dumb, and a lot of fun. He became a heavyweight Golden Glove Champion. He taught me a few things with the little time he was around. Damn, Skippy, I needed it. He said, "Always lead with your left, and the quickest way from point A to point B is a straight line. Learn to throw your jab fast, hard, and practice."

I practiced with weights in my hands. But before learning this, I had to learn how to wrestle. I had no teacher; this was on-the-job training. Black Pearl and I, a big ham-hock-eating son of a bitch, would fight every day. People came to watch the black and the white Puerto Rican nigger fight. We are the best of friends now, and Chucky had to beat his ass twice.

Public School 63—a gladiator school for real. Well, I had to do a lot of fighting. I never started it, but when pushed, I fought and fought hard. There came a day when I got into a squabble in the schoolyard at lunchtime; I punched a kid in the stomach. The little guy ran and told a female teacher.

She approached me and said, "It isn't nice. How would it feel if someone did it to you?"

She hit me in the stomach two times, buckling me over. I was the little guy this time.

I ran straight home to my mother and said to her, still crying, "Mommy, Mommy, a teacher punched me in the stomach."

"What happened?" she asked with concern.

"A little boy hit me, and I hit him back, and he went running crying to the teacher." She was a red-haired white lady; I didn't mention that, but I remember that very well. It was hardly any black teachers then, if any.

"Calm down," my mother said and let me get dressed.

My mother had pretty black wavy hair. I was wondering why she was taking so much time. Well, the outcome was nothing like I thought. The teacher, principal, my mother, and I met in the principal's office. There, the teacher said to my mother, "He was fighting with another child, and she broke it up, and I never hit him!

I screamed, "She's lying, Mommy!"

My mother smacked the little man in me out. That was the worst pain I ever felt—a white teacher lying to my mother, who was the world to me. This had a profound effect on me.

Now, I was mad—as mad as an eight-year-old could be. I watched a man count a lot of money and put it in a bag; then, he put it in the hole down the steps toward the basement, which led toward the backyard.

I circled around back, came up, stuck my hand inside that hole in the wall, and grabbed that bag! I tore through the backyard, stashed the bag with the cash, and then ran home with the notebook that was also in the hole.

As soon as I got home, a lot of people were there talking to my mother. I walked in with the book in hand; some man snatched it, asking, "Where's the money?"

After watching a professional liar, white, lying to my mother, I said, "I didn't see no money."

I wanted the book; I dropped the bag. We weren't liked around there. I remember my mom putting something in the tub and saying, "It was lye and had two long-handled pots to scoop it out on a motherfucker."

Yes, my mom was ready to go to war! Later, I got the bag and gave it to my mother instead of fighting.

We took a flight to 11-13 Washington Avenue and 1066 Street. My new school was Public School 132. Here, the first thing I noticed was the lunches—salads, vegetables, and desserts.

I was up every morning. My new teacher was not an upgrade either; she was very old and had a wart on her nose. Somehow, she got close to me. She taught me how to read and said, "If you read the newspaper every day, little words make big words, and you will have the history of tomorrow!"

That's what I did every day: read and sell the newspaper, smoke cigarettes, and drink coffee from nine to thirteen years of age. The killing of our president and all our black leaders, war, and the good soul music blasting! Shit, I needed to smoke and drink something. The last block was number running, and this new block was drugs and murders. Don't forget the children of the drug dealers and murderers. There, my brother's and sister's father was killed—thrown off the roof. I looked out the window in my room and saw him lying down there in the backyard. Maybe it was retaliation from the number man over his money, or maybe someone just wanted to get close to my mother—a strong, black, beautiful woman. Now, the children of these ruthless people were just as ruthless. They liked to rob, steal, and fight. I liked that; if you were scared, you couldn't show it.

When I asked my mother to help me with homework one day, she said, "I am learning with you." That was an awakening, and I must admit I was scared.

Well, hard times mean good times if you live to talk about the struggle and how you endured it. I guess my mother struggled with white label and Johnny Walker; she loved to party then, and I watched the kids. It's like a job: two brothers, two sisters, and my mother, who would sometimes be gone for two days. We were left hungry. I tried baking some bread with no eggs or milk; I'd use just flour. For grease, I used Dixie Peach hair grease, and they didn't like it even with syrup. We were PO! Hopefully, and most times, she came back with food and money. I'd eat, get paid, and then run out the door.

## THE STREETS

The streets, the sounds, and the smells were exciting to me. There was a Wonder Bread factory where you could smell the sweet scent of baked bread, like honey to a bear. New to the block, I'd see kids playing. *Um! The bread smells so good. I sure wish I could get me some,* I thought.

A kid asked, "Who are you?"

"Jimmy. Jimmy Holloway, just moved around here, OK!"

The kid said, "If you steal four sticks of butter from the supermarket, I'll show you how to get some bread!"

They all laughed. He seemed a little bit older, the rest about my age or younger. Once I secured the butter, C led us to the backyard and climbed up and across a few rooftops. There, he pointed, "Up the stairs through that door; take this bag; they're hot!"

From where I got my courage, I don't know, but I went up there through the door. I could feel the heat from the oven, and the sweet bread smell was wafting into the air as loaves came up on the conveyor belts.

I knocked about four or five loaves and ran back to the roof's edge, passed out the butter, tore the top off, stuck the butter down in the bread, and squeezed. My second heist—small but oh so tasty. Also, I made some new friends. We all did a lot of fun things, climbing in backyards, stealing when soda trucks came by, and whatnot. I thought I was fearless! And I guess that's why they liked me.

Once we went to Crotona Pool. Well, we all jumped in, and when I came out, M said, "Look at Jimmy's hair."

My afro had fallen really bad.

C said, "Oh, shit! He got that white boy hair: White Nigger Black Nigger (it hurt) but white!" They all laughed. Well, the joke was on me that day. Time to ask Mother about this.

As soon as I arrived home, I asked, "Ma, why is my hair like this and everyone else's not?"

Mom said, "They're just jealous. When you were a baby, I always brushed and greased your hair."

I thought, Yeah, right!

Well, the insults kept coming; even my own brother called me those names when he got mad. Anyway, what saved me from constant ridicule was Garry, K.K., and Jimmy, who was almost, well, whiter than me. Well, his mom, Nancy, was white.

We all played and climbed around together, but on this day, we all met outside, ready for today's adventure.

"Headcount, everyone is here! Let's go," C said.

"Where are we going?" I asked.

"You can't?"

"Why not?"

The reply was, "Well, we're going to do something we don't want anyone to know, and you probably won't want to do it."

I was curious and asked, "Do what?"

"We can't tell you. If you come, you must do it," C said.

"Well, I'm not scared. If you all do it, I will, too. When?" I asked.

"Right now, let's go!" C said.

Well, we went inside the abandoned storefront. It was filled with spark plugs and brakepads to mess each other up in the pass...? *This,* I thought, *is what I gave my oath to do.* This was a game-changer. I wasn't a victim; no, I was willing to participate!? That wasn't as painful as they wanted. They wanted to include my little brother, but I said, "No way, and I don't want to anymore!"

"Well, we're going to mess you up."

"Oh, well."

I fought the leader with all that I had. Although he was whipping my ass, I kept fighting. Then I heard a chuckle from the crowd; it was A. I turned and punched him in the mouth. I guess C softened me up, and it was easy for A to finish me. I staggered upstairs, exhausted as hell. And that was it for my mother.

We moved three blocks away to Fulton Avenue, 166 Street. It was much better, Third Avenue L, and terribly busy in a prosperous neighborhood. But we were still poor! I mean sugar water and fried fatback. We ate mayonnaise sandwiches, chicken backs, and rice.

Once, a store had a fire on Third Avenue; no, it was not me this time. After I went around to the back door, I got in and removed a box of magic markers. One of the Washington Avenue crew saw me.

I went around selling those magic markers to various stores. I made a pocketful of money and put it in my pants pocket. I had pants with a double lining and a hole in the pocket, so all my money fell to the bottom of my pants leg.

As I finished bumping them off and heading home, I was spotted by the Washington Avenue crew—about five of them. André said, "Yo, there's Jimmy; he took markers out of the fire; he got money!

"I've seen him selling stuff, yeah!" Carl said, coming to pat my pockets.

"I do not have any money," I said as he patted my pants pockets. "I don't have any money," I repeated.

He kept patting my pants pockets. "Jump up and down," he said.

Just like in the abandoned storefront, I jumped up and hauled ass up the block around the corner. All of them chasing me, my pants legs jingling and jangling. After an all-out sprint, I was home with the loot! Out of breath but safe, I laughed, then thought about André, his snitch ass. I thought to myself, *Not going to be running in fear every day.*

So, I started playing ball in the morning schoolyard, afternoon lunch, after school, and night gym. I came home so tired and stayed away from Washington Avenue as much as I could. It had been months since I last saw them. Then summer came, and I was coming out of the store. There they were, all six of them, still hanging together. Strange. I thought, *These guys still messing with each other, disgusting.* I guess they saw my disgust.

"Yo, Jimmy, you know you owe that money," one of them said.

I was scared. Then André O said, "Yeah, where's the money?" As he said it, he hit me in the back of my head.

I turned around and hit him with a right cross, which laid him out; his eyes rolled to the back of his head.

Everybody said, "Oh, shit."

The second time I heard, "Oh, shit," I was out... Less than three minutes, I was upstairs.

"Boy, what's wrong now?" my mama asked.

Yes, it seemed I was always getting into something. I had just turned eleven. This boy, André, hit me, and I punched him in the face. As soon as I had said that, someone was calling my mama outside. "Rosalyn, send your son down here." It was the boy's father, Asshole Senior, and everyone he could fit into or on top of that old station wagon from Washington Avenue.

Well, my mother yelled down, "Don't tell me what to do with my son." I think she cursed and then asked, "Jimmy, you want to go down?"

I didn't care; I had little choice. I went. As soon as I came out of the building, André came at me with a baseball bat his dad had given him. I ran into the street; this guy I learned, his name was Coot, I just met, yelled, "Jimmy, here," and threw me a stickball stick. I caught it as I ran; now it was even up.

Mom yelled down from the window, "Don't let him hit you with that baseball bat, Jimmy."

The thought never crossed my mind; everyone was outside. When I swung that stick and caught him on his hip, he let out a yelp and dropped the bat; I dropped my stick and jumped on his ass, raining lefts and rights, till he was down.

His father pulled me off him. My new friends were cheering, and I felt good! And tired! I felt welcomed on my new block; there were plenty of people to meet, but I remained cautious, not wanting to get too close. But these guys were different; they were into sports and games. There were three levels: the older guys, the guys a little younger than them, that be Neal, then Coot, who was instantly my friend, for he threw me the stickball stick.

Neal laughed a weird kind of laugh, shook my hand, and said, "Yo! You whipped that ass."

That night, I saw a lot of other people there, but Neal and Coot became my best friends. They were slightly older, but from what I'd been through and seen, I was not as happy to be their friend. There were much older guys, very intelligent. I loved listening to them talk about everything—politics, music. I mean, I was enlightened in many ways. Still reading the newspaper, I wanted the history of tomorrow.

And all of these guys were in college. I learned a lot from them and by reading their books.

This neighborhood was thriving; I quickly grew in recognition, and I was maturing physically. I was recognized as being fearless. Girls were taking notice of me, but I was into sports and politics—a lot was going on at that time. Poverty was present. Drugs were cheap. So were wine and liquor.

I smoked my first joint at eleven, cigarettes, and coffee at eight. Now, Neal and I had become good friends, talking to girls. When I wasn't with him, I was playing with Coot. This block was active, and I grew in knowledge, still reading the news. I admired the Black Panthers, especially after they killed John F. Kennedy, Robert, his brother, and then Martin and Malcolm. I was scared of so much violence happening in the world.

The things I just went through were still on my mind. Sports occupied much of my time—a way of escape. I played hard, and it took my mind away from the many questions I had. Once I played so hard, I was nodding. Ma looked at me and said, "Boy, what's wrong with you? You using dope?"

"No, Ma, you sure."

"No, Ma knows. Well, let me tell you, if you start sniffing that dope, then you will start skin-popping. Soon after that, you'll be mainlining, and you'll be hooked for life, just like Monkey Man."

"Oh, no, Ma."

Dope was running rampant; it was two dollars a bag, along with beer, wine, and liquor. The city was on fire with riots, looting, and police brutality. We were poor, and it was clearly visible in our lifestyle and appearance; my sneakers had holes, and the sock hung out. They used to say my shoes were thirsty. Neal and some of the older guys were wearing leather fronts, playboys. I wanted that!!

One night, there was a party at Trinity Church, and lots of girls were slow dancing. I was excited; I was close to twelve. Neal gave me a pair of pants and playboys for the night. Wow! I went home, got dressed, played some records, and practiced some steps and lyrics of my favorite songs. I was ready in my playboya. I came down just in time to see Neal, Sam (who they called Shorty), Joe Willie, and Stinky Casanova. "Come on, Stinky," I cried.

"Hold on, I'll be there," Neal said.

"What time are you going to the party?" I asked.

"Jimmy, I'll meet you at the party because we are getting ready to do something. I'm not sure you're going to be down."

Hmmm, this sounds familiar, I thought.

"Well, Jimmy, it can't be worse than what you had experienced on Washington Avenue."

Well, I wanted to be down. So, I said, "Whatever, I'm down."

"Ok, come on," Neal said.

I followed him upstairs to the third floor, 11-29, an abandoned apartment with only a candle to light the room. There, sitting in a circle around a mayonnaise jar of ice water, Shorty Casanova and Joe Willie.

"Ahh, I know! Why you bring this motherfucker up here?" Willie said.

"I don't like anyone knowing my business. I'm not a fucking snitch," I said.

"Fuck that," Stinky said.

"He's here now. Pass them bags; sit down, Jimmy. Here, you know what this is?" Neal asked as he took a snort and made a little grimace.

"Yeah, dope," I said.

"Yeah. We just sniff it. Get nice before going to the party. Here, take a little one-on-one."

How could I say no? Well, after the bags were empty, we walked three blocks to the party. I remember nothing but darkness, silence, and how I got home. Well, one thing I was sure of: there was no display or talk of sex of any kind. But somehow, I felt something was taken from me, yet I was a willing volunteer once again. I guess right about that time, Mom gave me that talk about drugs, and her words rang true. For a little over a month, instead of sniffing, they graduated to skin popping. That was my cue to say, "Nawh! I'm not down," then walk away from a good friend.

One thing I decided was not to follow others, and I was trying to follow no one but myself. I lead, not follow; for anyone to follow, you had to bring something, have something. I originally brought my jeans with bleached holes and patches; I was handsome in bum clothes. If I had something new, I'd be scared to go outside; I didn't much like attention. Plus, it seems there was always something to fight about.

Soon, I found interest in girls. I started fighting less and playing more. Ahh, yes, girls! They were fun to kiss; I had a technique while I was kissing them. I would inhale their breath, creating a dizzy feeling. Hence, the song "take my breath away." I grew to be a great kisser sought after by many.

## PIMPING INC.

Here I am on the bus heading to Fort Dix, New Jersey. Two days after my eighteenth birthday, I enlisted in the United States Army with my Michael Jackson Afro, hoping to gain skills and knowledge to be a better man and see the world from a new angle.

My time was running out, and my choices were limited. The weight of the world was on my shoulder, meaning that my world and everything that I grew to love the first-born male.

My grandma came here to New York from Sumter, South Carolina, hoping to make it here without education and skills; the only jobs available were cleaning white folk's asses. They were three strong, beautiful black women—Grams, Tutie, and Mom.

Grams named me "Bookie" because I loved books, and they loved them some Bookie! These were the women who spoiled me, wiped tears from my eyes, and taught me how to be the man that women wanted! Books, TV, and the streets taught me the rest.

I was reading the newspaper, and drinking coffee, smoking cigarettes at the age of ten, reading Donald Groin's Iceberg Slim, Whoreson, and Trick Baby. When watching television, I loved watching gangsters—Capone, Frank Nitty, and It Takes a Thief with Alexander Munday, Super Fly, Costello, Gotti, Nicky Barnes stealing, strong arm robbery, and drug dealers. Most of these people I admired when I was young died or went to prison for a long period of time; that was not for me: oh, hell to the nawh! But pimping? I never heard of pimping getting twenty years. I was already eye candy for ladies: that light, curly, sandy blond hair. The girls said I was nasty and fresh! My mama said, "You not going to keep a woman with just your looks."

So I started playing pimp games and played them with my main man Al Sabrina Mckelvey in Clark Junior High School. I met up with Al and told him about my idea of pimping. I was Sweet Pimping Jim! Inc.

That made me feel good, didn't cost anything, and I needed a friend since it was dangerous out here. A couple of things keep you from getting in trouble—one is being funny and a jokester; Al was that, and I kept a good knuckle game and kept it tuned by snatching flies out of the air.

In school one day, I was at the back of the class talking to a girl in the hallway with the door cracked. This idiot kicked the door, locking me out, and also smashed my finger. In pain, I ran to the front door and banged on it violently, screaming, "Open open!!!

I saw who did it. Now sitting like he didn't do anything. I think I knew he was a member of the Black Spade, but my pain said, "Smack the fuck out of him," and I listened to my pain. I smacked him clean out of his chair, and he screamed, "I'm going to get the spades."

"Get who you want," I said.

It seemed like they were out in the hallway, for as soon as he left, the Black Spade group was coming in through the back door and the front door, and they started moving out the desk and chairs.

I was sitting in the middle, and they surrounded me. One came walking toward me, and I stood up.

He asked, "Why you stood up?"

I said, "Everybody else is standing, and I have to see a nurse. Your man smashed my finger in the door."

If talking didn't work, my hand would be on the chair, swing me a path out, but security came, and the leader said, "We'd handle this later."

From then on, I was on their radar. And they were on mine. When I see them, I go in the opposite direction. I had nothing to worry about running with a gang, only if I was the leader. One or two, three, a crowd draws a lot of attention. Well, the Black Spade pressured me to join and even offered me my own division—somewhat undercover and only having to show up if they had a battle. Me and Al agreed, but we never showed up. Grundy dirty, im not with that, terrorizing, robbing, even some rapes. Nope, not for me.

## SWEET PIMPING JIM INC.

Al said, "Am a million-dollar pimp.

"Well, we all started writing our names with magic markers all over schools, we developed handshakes, playing, and dressing Kool; you know, toothpicks and handkerchiefs in our back pockets. We shared everything! We had little, but what we had, we shared, we talked like we got money and business happening. One thing that I liked about Al was that he could lie with a straight face... as he said, he had a pool table in his basement.

I had only known him for about a year, and when I met him, he said he had a pool table in his basement; when I'd go to his house, I'd always suggest playing some pool, and he would always put it off and make excuses. One day, I happened to go down to the basement with him for something. I guess he forgot, and I saw a miniature pool table with marbles!!! We laughed so hard at that moment. My man, Al Million Dollar Pimp, I wish I could write more about him... he died at 26 in a motorcycle accident.

Well, I continued with this pimping idea, recruiting Rudy Ray Moore's Last Poet's jokes, making oneself the most exciting, funny, strong, confident, and sure of yourself with the ability to create something out of nothing. I guess being poor helps you with this ability, being there's nothing to work with. I found pain and hunger to be great teachers, so I started thinking of myself as special, walking a little differently, talking with great plans, and keeping an air about myself, always lying, saying I gotta do this or dat. One Easter, I was in Junior High School. I was ashamed to go outside, for I had nothing new to wear!

## GRANDMA

Grams said, "Boy, you don't need no new clothes, just clean clothes!

We washed my favorite Wrangler jeans, bleached me a white shirt, and my Converse sneakers. Grams made some starch from flour and pressed and starched my jeans and shirt and creased them so sharp that they'd cut you.

She put Goya olive oil on my face and hair and then said, "Go on out there; you can hang with the best of them." I always remembered her words, and this is still true today!

Sitting on the bus, I reflect on my life in the City of New York, a city of players, gangsters, and drug dealers, winos, dope users, not to forget the car thieves; this was and still is big business, and it was also a lot of fun for me.

When I got my first job, Al, who was 17, and I was a messenger at 7 West 57$^{th}$ Street, between Sixth Avenue J, and thought I would find money on the street. Well, at 22, there was a whole lot of money, but none in the streets.

When I received my first paycheck, I was stunned; I couldn't believe it. I said to my boss, "Boss, check this out. I'm missing hours here, look! Oh, no, that's a full workweek." I thought, *I'm here in the richest part of the world, and there's millions all around now (HOW DO I GET IT?).*

In the late sixties and seventies, everybody was smoking weed, and New York had it good. I heard "A monkey can't sell bananas," but I was strong-willed and planned on changing the game! So, I was a messenger/loose joints, and I rode my bike to work—a green Schwinn kept me in shape.

I peddled my loose joints in Central Park, but the money was in Bryant Park.

At lunchtime, we'd roll up one jay right there in the park (Panama Gold, Red Kush. And Chunky Black) the world seemed to be lit! By 12:30, loose joints would turn into quarter ounces, and the clientele grew! I met many celebrities; one was Calvin Lockhart's son, Leslie. He was getting weight from me, sometimes on consignment.

Once, he was late with the payment. He had a nice studio on 57th Street and 6th Avenue.

"Yo! Les, where's my money, man?" I asked.

"Jimmy, my man, things are a little tight. I'll hit you next week."

"Yeah, yeah, you say that next week when you short. Man, ain't your father rich?" I said.

Les said, "Yeah, but he just gave me an allowance. I gotta make it on my own."

"Yo! Les, what you have now? Something, I can't tell my peeps I'm short again. They won't like that," I said.

"Hey, look! I've got this embossed cowhide briefcase... at least a quick thousand," Les said.

Although I was poor, I loved expensive things of quality. "Ok, this time, movie star, next time, have my cash!

Les replied, "Well, all-star's head, arms, and two legs. Five points and see you can shine."

"Yeah, I hope you shine next week."

The briefcase was beautiful, and I bought a new pair of shoes to match it. I was the koolest messenger you've ever seen; hard to believe that I was that! Maybe a courier. I made sure every day I came to work; I was fly, clean, and smelling good. I'd catch everyone's eyes, and I loved that GQ look, go to Macy's, Blooming Dales and get that free sample of cologne; Grey Flannel, Polo, and Pierre Cardin, when I delivered; yes packages, envelopes I became a worker of that company. I memorized the names to grab attention, and so I flattered the receptionist: I would say, "Hey, Rob Goldman here? I work in color restoration. I need his signature on a few items. Is he in? I'd continue, "We could possibly do lunch after I speak with him."

The reply would be, "Yes, down the hall and make a right, and the second door on the right, thanks!"

On my brief journey, I'd riffle through pockets and desk drawers, taking petty cash, watches, and wallets left in coats, expensive pens (Mel Blanc pens), get my signature, and be out.

# Chapter Two
# That Caddy Top of the Line

My messenger pay wasn't that much, but the fringe benefits made up for that! This soon progressed to stealing cars on my routes; sometimes, I'd see cars with keys in the ignition. Once, I tried a VW Bug, a standard car before; I figured I'd get it started. However, every time I put it in gear, it would lurch and then cut off three times. Finding no luck with it, I gave up.

Well, I always come to work early to give me plenty of time. I believe when you're early, you're on time; when you're on time, you're late, plus the early bird gets the worm! This morning, I came an hour early. There were cars backed up in the parking lot. The attendant was so busy and had a few cars left with keys in ashtrays, under the mat, or on top visors. Guess what I see? Yes, a Caddy Sedan Deville. Well, I got it started, but I didn't know how to release it, so I applied the emergency brake. I got out and asked a chauffeur, "How and where is the release button for the emergency brake?"

He said, "There is no release button. You just step on the brakes and put the car in gear, and it releases automatically."

"Oh! Okay, thank you," I said and went back to the car. I started the car, put it in reverse, backed that Caddy out of the driveway, and turned the radio on WBLS. I wasn't going to work that day, so I headed back to the Bronx. Funny, I was thinking of getting my crew to go for a car ride; I knew this would make me a leader around the block.

Bryant Avenue and 1075 Street. Who is the cat driving the Cadillac, dressing so fly, keeping the best weed? Well, in the trunk of the Caddy was a case of fine champagne. I had the keys styled with it, dressing to match the car. I parked the car and went to work. Later, I went home in a style that nobody could tell if it was not your car. Once my mother saw me in that car, she said, "Boy, what are you doing with that car?"

I said, "Mom, my boss gave it to me to deliver packages for my job." I knew it wasn't true. Well, I didn't live with her. I had my own place, a room in a private house.

One beautiful Saturday afternoon, I was all dressed in white tennis shorts. I picked up my man, Larry, and said to him, "Let's go play some ball, puff some of this good shit."

"My nigga, you always got it good," he said. "We riding?"

I replied, "You know that. Let's go to Crotona Park, Kool."

I loved playing ball and boxing, and I was very good. While driving to the park on this beautiful summer day, at a red light, guess who pulled up beside me? New York's finest policemen! They pulled right up beside me, looked at me, and asked, "Is that your car?"

I said, "No, it's my boss's car." Then, my brain started to race, and it went into warp drive, remembering my man Al, Sabrina Mckelvey, who died; how he could lie with a straight face and had details and didn't show any emotion. *This would be huge if I could pull this off,* I thought.

The officer said, "Pull over. License and registration."

"Oh, I left my wallet in the gym locker," I replied.

"Yeah, right. This vehicle has been reported stolen. I'm taking you in," the officer said.

The officer moved to the radio to inform headquarters about the stolen car. I was still a juvenile on one-year probation. At the time of the verdict, the judge told me, "Do not let me see you here again!"

As the officer moved, I realized if they radioed in, I'd be caught, and they'd find out I had stolen a few more cars since then. The last one was a 1975 AMC Matador, rented this time by my friend, Bubbe, who was riding shotgun.

I learned never to ride by the police and to avoid them like the plague. It was around 9:30 pm. Up and over on the east side of Bronx Wood, I spotted the police sitting in their car at the intersection. I wondered if I could pass them at the light because I didn't want to be caught there on red.

So, I sped up, but before I could cross it, it turned yellow. It became certain that I wouldn't be able to make it now; it was red. I tried to stop the car, and it made a little screech. The cops looked over and yelled, "Hey!!"

I said, "Hold on, Bubba!" And I floored it while taking off my seatbelt, and they were coming whup! Whup! When I stopped the car, we jumped and made a run for it to be ready. I floored for three blocks, spun the car, and threw it in the park while it was still moving. During this effort, I belled and skinned my knee. However, I got up and ran to the nearest alleyway. I heard the dogs barking in the next yard, so I sought a place to hide under. I squeezed myself into and under the first two steps of the back porch stairs.

While the cops' siren blared, I saw flashlights shine and cops talking. The lady came to the back door and asked one of the cops, "Is everything alright?"

The cop asked the lady, "Did you hear anything?"

"No, No," she said.

I was right there, hiding under the stairs, sweating, my heart beating so loud that I thought for sure they heard it! I was not so religious or spiritual, but all the time, holding my silver chain with rubies and a saint on it, I prayed then so hard. "Please, God, please don't let them find me, please, I'll be good. I'll go into the military, God, please," I said repeatedly in my head as they shined the lights under the stairs; it just missed me. Bubba got caught, and true to my word, I enlisted.

Yes, I escaped that time, the crimes of the city. *They almost caught me,* I thought. Right at that moment, a female voice broke into my thoughts, "Is this seat taken?"

"No, but I am," I said in a huff, disturbed by her! But when I looked up at her, she was fine, well, physically. She was what all men want, but I've seen plenty of even finer women drooling for me. I've always been a little choosey, no sugar. "I mean, I signed up. And now I'm on my way to boot camp."

She said, "Aww. You gonna let them cut off all that beautiful hair? You'll still be handsome, though. I live close to Fort Dix. Maybe I'll come see you there."

"Little girl, you don't know what you are messing with. I'm dangerous," I said.

"You don't look like danger. I'm not scared, by the way," she said.

"Well, here's my full name. Look me up there—Jimmy J. Holloway."

Later, I forgot her name, but she remembered mine; she wrote it on her arm and waved goodbye as she exited. I didn't think much about her and shut my eyes. I continued shortly after arriving at my destination. I got my haircut, shave, uniforms, and an M-Sixteen Auto intense training started.

One Saturday, in the early afternoon, while cleaning my weapon, I heard Holloway being yelled at by many. I looked out of the window, and I saw six soldiers standing there with a gorgeous girl. She waved as the others came to the windows; all were like, "Damn!" I wasn't so excited; I was used to women wanting to get with me; shit, I'm Harlem-born, Bronx-raised.

I met Pvt. Philly Kennedy. He was like he had never seen anything finer. I told him, "I'll bring back her panties for you to sniff if you watch my weapon while I'm gone with her." I went to town to rent a room and tore that pussy out of the frame!

# Chapter Three
# Army Life and My First Working Girl!

As I came down to wait for the cab, the six guys were waiting, wanting to open the door for her. "Guys, guys, I got this," I said. It seemed they wanted her more than me! Well, I checked in overnight.

She said, "You thought I wasn't coming!"

"Well, it completely slipped my mind." I was so busy with training, and that was all I had to say as we entered the hotel room.

I was eighteen with a military ID. So, it was my first. I suggested a beer, but she said, "Well, I have some weed "Acapulco Gold."

What!!! Her response just shocked me.

We puffed and got naked. Her body was shining and smelling of cocoa butter. My dick was harder than Chinese Arithmetic; what seemed like an hour was probably less than ten minutes. I thought about my weapon, which had to be turned into a .357 Smith & Wesson Magnum.

Back at the barracks, I was greeted by my comrades, and they said, "Yo! You brought back the panties?"

"No, I forgot, but what are you going to do with panties? You want some of that good, good. Oh, Yeah! No doubt!" I said.

"Well, yeah, me too," Kennedy said.

Well, right then and there, my pimping skills came into play. Shit, I've only seen this girl twice. She wants nails, feet, and hair done, and a facial shit! Here's a way to get this money! I said, "Okay, who got a hundred? Shit, for the hundred I got, I must go first, sure! The rest, which was two others, was half price. Fifty a piece causes the Muhamad-Foreman fight tonight, two of you! So, we will make it a night to remember."

Well, with the skills I acquired from reading books and a dream, it was easy to convince her. It paid off, and I gave her the proceeds of the money I made and explained to her; of course, she accepted as she needed to buy weed and rolling paper. Kennedy and I rolled joints, sold liquor, and made a couple of hundred. Before I graduated from boot camp, I was an above-average soldier.

Back at home, Mom got shitted on by her punk husband. He also molested my sisters and caused them homelessness. He couldn't wait for me to leave so he could do what he pleased. When Mom came and told me what had happened to her, I gave her all the money I had, and that wasn't enough; I wanted to kick his ass. All the way in, somehow, that news affected me. Unfortunately, I got sick with the

Swine Flu, fever, and headaches, and two people died. I suffered three days in the infirmary, and I was so sick that I received an honorable discharge; it should have been medical.

So, here I was at the port authority, Times Square in New York in January—New York where I belong, still sick in my uniform. I found my way to my grandma's house; my mother and aunt were there; they nursed me back to health. I had a fifth of Bourbon from Germany in about a month, and I was well.

When I got better, I thought to look for this punk who ravaged my family, but first things first. I needed to find a job, get my mother an apartment, and then gather up my sisters and brothers. This man really fucked up my family, being it was fragile anyway.

My mother and I got the apartment and slept on springs with clothes on it till we got mattresses. My baby brother got lost in the village with the gays, little sis gay, and big sis! The brother next to me stayed in school. Still, all was damaged, and repairing it all seemed difficult.

I met a girl. She was pretty, coffee-colored, with a flashing smile and two kids; she was also struggling. I thought of a diamond in the rough. One day, she told me, "The kids are with their grandma for the weekend, and I've two tabs of blotter, and I want to do it with you."

"Cool!!" I said. Let me tell you that was the best night of my life!! Even now, I mean tripping in color explosions nonstop, multiple orgasms, lots of kissing. I woke up in love, meaning she had gotten up and made breakfast and served me in bed. After last night, I was so hungry. She brought the plate to me, and it contained cheese grits, eggs, and beacon within mins. I had fallen off to sleep.

When I awoke, she had a fresh pair of Magic Johnsons. She said, "It's a magic night, and you're my Magic Man."

That's fine with me. Yeah, Magic Man, I was walking on sunshine.

I was still with my mom, and I told her, "I think I am going to be living with this girl."

"What? Why?" my mom asked.

"Well, she brought me these new sneakers, breakfast in bed, not to mention the unmentionable," I replied.

My mom said, "Boy, what's so special about that? She ain't do nothing special."

Having listened to her, I just smiled. It seemed the next week came fast. I went over to her house; the kids were gone, and the lights were out. I mean, Con Ed shut off! We used candles and jumped lights from the hallway. She said, "I want to ask you something, ok?

I said, "Shoot."

She continued, "You know where I can make some money, some track or stroll?"

I was stunned. Something I dreamed about and fantasized about was being offered. Of course, I said yes. I know. Now, back at Fort Dix, I had just met that girl and never kissed, but this was different.

"You ready," I asked.

"Yeah, this outfit good?"

"Oh, yeah." I smiled. "Let's go downtown where the money is—42$^{nd}$ Street, ok?"

On the train ride down, I was trying to develop a system. If she got into a car, I would have safety measures in place, and if that happened, I would follow. I said to her, "I'll meet you right where you left me. If you go into a building or hotel, leave a piece of gum out in front of the door."

I tell you, I was probably more scared than she was. I wasn't afraid as much as the first time in Fort Dix; I hardly knew her, but this girl felt different to me. I sorta had feelings for her; well, she's poor, I'm poor, maybe this is a way out.

Arriving at 42$^{nd}$ Street, still in daylight, I suggested walking down Eighth Avenue toward 34$^{th}$ Street, but before reaching there, she caught a trick; they stopped in a store and then proceeded down the street. I watched from across the street. I never took my eyes off them while trying to remember the details of the trick; the YMCA was in the direction they were walking. I surmised that was where the trick was taking her. She saw me; actually, I was in the elevator with them. I saw the floor and room number, so there was no need for the gum. I still listened at the door. The tingling of her bracelets echoed in my mind as I caught the elevator down to the lobby and waited until she came down within twenty minutes. She had a smile on her face and said, "Let's get some cigarettes."

"Newport's coming up."

"How much?"

"Fifty dollars, here's twenty-five."

"That's Kool. I'm going to make more."

"Yes, this is good. Let's take a break. Smoke a joint and do the math before the next one.

"I'm proud of you. Good job." I also suggested she stay with the white ones.

The joint and cigarettes eased my mind, and the tingling of her bracelets disappeared. I assumed my position, and it wasn't long before she attracted another fish. This guy was short and black, contrary to all that I had told her the conversation they had I wasn't aware of; from looking on, it seemed to be a bad choice and a waste of time, but time would tell.

I kept a close watch on them as they walked up 38<sup>th</sup> Street toward Ninth Avenue. *What's there? This guy can't have an apartment here,* I thought as they went into the building. Once they entered the building, I followed and heard them walking up ahead. I waited on the ground floor; the sound of her bracelets tingled rapidly, but not for long before I heard someone bounding down the stairs and out the front door. I hollered, "Yvonne, you alright?" I hollered again, "Yvonne, you alright?"

"No, Magic, no!" she yelled back.

I took off out of the building, seeing the trick walking back toward Eighth Avenue. I quickly crossed the street, keeping my eyes on him as I closed the distance. I caught his ass right at the corner of 40th Street. I cracked him with my fist to the head, then grabbed him and threw him up against the corner with my elbow against his throat. I searched his pockets for money but found nothing; I felt the knife and didn't think anything of it. I asked him, "Where's the money?"

He replied, "I ain't got none! I gave it to her."

I punched him in the face, and the stubble got up and ran. As he ran, I yelled at him, "If I see you again, I'll whip your ass again."

It was time for me to get back to my girl and find out what happened. I walked back toward 38th Street. I saw her coming out of the building and saw her face. She was a little shaken, but no blood.

"What happened?" I asked her.

She said, "When we got to the top floor, he pulled out a knife and told me to pull down my pants. He was so scared that he came fast and ran down the stairs right out of the building."

I asked her, "Are you alright?"

She said, "Yeah."

I told her, "I searched for him and felt the knife, but I was looking for money, and there was none."

This incident scared me. Well, quickly, I felt the danger of the profession. We needed to try something else, maybe dancing in a peep show; there were plenty at that time: Show World, Peep Land, and Black Jacks. Black Jacks was the one we got lucky at. The manager's name was Billy, but he worked for an Italian named Ricco. I knew she had to please Ricco because Billy, being Black, liked white girls and made it hard for Black girls to get on the schedule; they had to please him or give him a cut of what they made. I didn't like that and tried to appear menacing whenever I showed up. I had fallen for the girl, unlike the others, plus she had kids. I felt she was risking her life to feed and protect them, so I would help and protect her.

I worked days in the garment district, and she worked at night and on weekends. Money was pouring in, the kids were happy, and I had a car, a dog, and a fish tank. I had clothes and jewelry, and life was good in the first year. The second year, however, got real; cocaine appeared!

During our night together one weekend, she introduced me to cocaine after work. Her voice changed, raspy and sexy, and she said with a slow drawl, "Try some."

I was hooked. Every week on the weekend, we'd freak out on each other, licking and sucking; the cocaine heightened my sexual desire and maybe lessened hers. Soon, she started saying I wanted too much, and she was often tired. She'd say wait for me to want you. Shit! She was taking too long.

While watching the kids as she worked, I made a few friends. You know they'd see me in the supermarket bringing bags out to the car. So, this is how I met Michelle. She was a fine, chocolate, juicy-lipped girl, and I'd talk to her for hours and hours. There were no two-way calls at that time, so when someone called, the phone was busy.

So, one day, while on the phone talking to Michelle, my girl came home early. When I heard the door, I hung up!

She said, "Oh, no, don't hang up now. You've been on the phone for two hours. Don't say you've been talking to Coot, my friend. Go out, or I'm going back out! Well, shit, after babysitting all night, I was ready, plus hearing her mouth, I was out! I called Michelle up from a pay phone.

"What's up?" Michelle asked.

I told her what just happened and I had no place to stay the night. I noticed she had a nice apartment.

Michelle said, "I have a man but haven't seen him in 3 months."

"Well, if it's alright, I'd leave in the morning. Here, put this in the freezer. I'd like crisp, cold Heineken with your juicy lips," I said.

Later, after a beer and a joint, I found out all her lips were juicy. Soon after tagging that ass, I fell asleep only to awake with the light shining in my face and a tall brother with a beige snorkel on! He had his hand in his pocket. He said to me, "Get up."

"Ok," I said as I searched for my pants that I had peeled off in drunk passion.

He lit up a joint, took a strong poke, and then asked me, "You want some?"

I said, "No. I just want to get out of here."

He said, "You need carfare?"

"No," I said.

"What did she tell you about me?:" he asked.

I replied, "She said she hasn't seen you for a few months."

He asked, "Did she tell you I'm 'Loco.'"

Well... my life kinda flashed before me. We were on the sixth floor. "Nawh, man. She didn't say that. Look, I would like to get out of here!!" I said.

Well, when I got out of there, I went home at about 3:30, badly mad at my girl for forcing me out. I almost died, but I couldn't tell her that. But from then on, the sex kind of died, and the cocaine increased.

So, with her schedule working as a dancer and me working at Jordach Apparel, our time together got shorter. I became bored, so I met another woman who loved fucking me, but she was bisexual and wanted a threesome with me, but she did not have another girl.

Oh, by the way, when I woke up, I called Michelle and asked her, "Are you alright?"

She said, "Yes, I'm ok."

I asked, "Why did you open up the door without waking me up?"

She said, "When he knocked, he told me, 'Open this door now, or else I'll shoot the lock off.'"

"Oh, I see. What's up with him now?"

She said, "He's gone, and he took his things, so he's not coming back, I guess!"

I said, "Good." Then I asked her, "Have you ever had a woman?"

She replied, "No, but I wouldn't mind if she ate my pussy!!"

I said, "Sure, that's what she wants to do."

"Who," she asked.

I said, "Deb."

"Ok. When?" she asked.

I said, "Soon. I'll set it up."

I told Deb I had a girl who was willing to join in. Listening to this news, she got so excited and asked, "When?"

I replied, "Soon, but I have to plan this just right."

I was thinking, *I don't want to get caught.* I must admit I was more excited than they were (I just didn't want to get caught!).

Two days later, it was on. I brought a six-pack of champagne and a dime sack of Lamb's Bread, picked Deb up, and took her to Michelle's house. Oh, yeah, every man's fantasy—two women licking, sucking any and everything, till the wee hour… then the morning comes, you got to go home and face the music, and it was loud. As soon as I walked in, my girl was up, I mean, not sleeping all night, waiting for me; she said, "I know you were out there fuckin some bitch!! Go on and lie. I seen you drive by. Where were you? Don't lie!"

I was dead tired and didn't have the energy to create one. I didn't plan on getting caught. My friends said I should never admit, lie, or deny. This is what sets me apart from the rest. Scorpio will tell you the truth. So I started saying, "Yes, baby, I was, but it wasn't just one woman; it was two, honey. I want you to know I don't care for them. It was just a fantasy. I love and want you and you only."

"Did you fuck any in their ass?" she asked.

"Honey, I don't wanna talk about it?" I said.

"No. Did you?"

"No!!"

"Why?"

"Well, there was too much pussy to think about butthole, honey. Please forgive me. It was my fantasy. I'm sorry. I want and love you."

"Well, I have a fantasy too, yeah? I wanna get fucked by five men!"

"Whoa! I hope I don't find out."

"OH! You won't 'cause you got to get out!"

Well, I didn't leave right away, but things were never the same. It was a lot of pain leaving someone you loved for many years, especially the children. On top of that, my mother was going to Miami for a job, telling me to take care of things while she was gone. I was heartbroken and homeless.

In snot and tears, Mom said, "Son, it be alright when a woman leaves you. I want you to celebrate and drink champagne, for a better one will come along. Never liked her anyway."

So, I wiped away the tears, feeling good about myself. My mom always had good advice. Like when I was eleven, she said, "Sniffing them duce bags, soon you'll be skin popping, then you mainline."

I only sniffed twice. Only my close friends continued into that dark place. She wasn't wrong then. So, I dried my eyes, put on a smile, and said goodbye to my mama. Well, the sounds of New York were silent; even the sun didn't seem to be shining as bright. Not wanting to appear homeless, I asked Sgt., boss of a poolroom and gambling spot on Third Avenue and 166 Street, "Can I leave my bags there till I find somewhere to put them? I just got put out."

Sargent was a short, bow-legged man who smoked cigars and talked with a deep, raspy voice. I guess he was in the military long ago; now, he was just a gambler and shit-talker. He said to me, "Hey, kid, if you help me keep the place clean and run some errands for me, there's a bed up there," He pointed to the ceiling. Shit! "You be here all the time anyway."

"Yeah, you're right. Thanks, Sgt."

There I would be every day and night, shooting craps—Ce lo, Blackjack, Poker, and Pool; I'd gotten pretty good at all games, and I started winning. With the winnings, l started stepping up my game, plus I was getting horny as hell. It had been a couple of months now since the breakup. I was still mad, and I wasn't going back, but I recalled a girl who always had eyes for me; this girl lived across the street from my ex. I couldn't remember her name, but I was horny, so I went there. I knocked on the door. When she opened the door, her eyes lit up the moment she saw me.

"Hey, baby," I said, reaching and embracing her. She was scantily dressed as I squeezed her tightly. "How you been?" I whispered in her ear, blowing and softly kissing her neck. My Dick was harder than times of twenty-nine.

"Where you been? I haven't seen you in a while?" she said.

"Yeah, we broke up. I stay crosstown now," I said as I ran my hands over her ass and hips while walking her toward the bedroom. "You locked the door?" I asked. Shit, I learned from last time. It's been two months, and I began to savor that ass slowly. I liked to lick it before I stuck it. Just as I began to stick it a few times, there was a knock on the door. "Who's that?" I whispered.

She said, "I do see someone else sometimes, but I ain't expecting him today."

"Well, you're not home," I said. And I continued banging that ass while he knocked. The knocking stopped for an hour, then started right up again. His knocking like that made me stay hitting the pussy till the wee hours. After being caught with my pants down in the last incident, I didn't fall asleep in a woman's house after sex anymore. So, we talked through the night. I told her, "I stay in a club and need some money to buy some cocaine and start my business."

"How much you need?" she asked.

"A thousand," I said.

"Why so much?" she asked. "You couldn't do it with five hundred?"

"No, for there's scales and other items I need. You got to do things right or not at all."

"Ok. I'll give you a thousand tomorrow."

Now I really couldn't sleep. The morning took a long time to come. I lay there till she was fully dressed. "Come on," she said.

"Ok," I said, dressing quickly.

We took a cab to the bank. "I'll wait here at Wendy's," I said to her.

Soon, she was back. "You want it under the table or over?"

I said, "Slide it to me under the table." She did. "Nice," I said.

"So, when will I see you?"

"Soon, as I score."

"Ok, later."

POW! I was out like I stole something. I checked the envelope; it was eight hundred and four-fifties. I walked back uptown slowly, considering my next move. Once on the block, I ran into Kenney. "Yo! Kenny, a girl just gave me a thousand dollars."

"What!!!" Kennedy said with shock on his face and in his tone.

I showed him. "The price of this dick is going up now. I'm looking to score some coke. Let's ask Craig."

Craig was an older brother whose father ran numbers. Mr. Bunny, and you better call him that. Craig works in one of the number joints. "Let's go! Jimmymack."

"What up, Craig! Yo, Craig. Can you get me a quarter of coke?"

"You know how much that costs?" Craig said.

"No, but can this get it?" I said, flashing the cash at him.

His eyes bulged. "Oh, yeah, that's more than enough. Let me make some calls."

Soon, I was hooked up with two brothers; the oldest one was Cozy, and the youngest was Fox, around my age. I put the money in Cozy's hands. It took a while, but he returned with a chunk of coke, which looked like ivory soap. "My man, magic, the way you put that money in my hand shows your trust in me. Look here." He pulled out a large stack of bills. "Being you roll like that, I'm hook you up, bow! That's

how I'm going to hit you! Yo, Cozy, that's a strong solid."
We shook hands, and I was ready to leave. Fox walked me
to the door and said, "Magic, there's a Kool spot on the
Concourse, player, called The Recovery Room. Stop by."

"Sounds good, but later," I said.

Things started to pick up now. I was making ends meet,
still stinging from the breakup. She didn't think I was
enough for her. This time, no more mister nice guy making
money now. I had a room I rented from my grandma; yes,
she wanted that money. Sometimes, she had a girl there,
poking her lips out to me, pointing to the girl. I smiled, went
into the room, and lay down. The next day, well-rested
playing Luther and getting in the groove, I suddenly heard a
knock on the door; it was the girl who lived upstairs.

"Yes!" I said.

"My sister asked me to give you this." She said, handing
me an envelope.

"Ok, thanks," I said, taking the envelope from her hand.

I looked at her phat ass as she walked away, wishing she
was giving me something. But I remember her sister, looking
down at me from the window above; oh, yes, her name was
Joan! But she had a man and two kids. *She is a Pretty
Chocolate woman. But no, I can't go through this again*, I
thought.

I opened the envelope. The letter read: "Hi, my name is Joan. I hear you playing that music. It seems you're in some breakup pains. My kids' father stays here, but we aren't together. Here's my number—4256659. Call!"

Me, I will, but not now.

Things started picking up. The coke was raw, and that's the way I sold it. My name started to ring up and down Third Avenue, making some cash. I used my grandma's house as my stash, plus I hit grandma with some cash. She doesn't see anything, knows nothing, Friday nights big, poker games cee lo, this night while playing cards, Vance walked in and said, "Yo, Jimmy! I got a girl for you."

"Man, I don't need no girl!! I need some money," I said.

"Man, that's what I'm talking about. She is looking for a pimp!" Vance said.

"What? Now you're talking about. Where's she?" I said.

"Outside, come on, BJ. This Jimmy is the one who I told you about," Vance said.

"Hi, my male friends call me Jimmy, but you can call me magic," I said.

"Magic, I like that. Can you work magic?" BJ said.

"Well, you listen, I'm tellin' you, then if you're ready, I show you," I said.

"Well, start talking, for I need some money like yesterday," BJ said.

"See, Jimmy, I told you," Vance said.

"Let me hold a little something, Jimmy."

"Yeah, I guess fine fees are in order. Let's step inside. Drinks on me. Come, BJ. Let's have a drink and get to know each other," I said.

"OK," she said.

"After you," I said. I checked out her ass as she walked in. Kind of flat, but she was cute.

We talked for a while over drinks. "Now, let's see whether she has skills in the head department. Look, I'm going to the bathroom. I leave the door open; when it's cool, you come in after," I said.

It was less than two minutes before she came in. My dick was already out, semi-hard, anticipating a blow job from BJ. She didn't disappoint; she quickly grew my penis to its full size in a matter of seconds. With her hands reaching for my balls, she cupped and pulled back, gently stroking and moaning. She really had impressive skills.

# Chapter Four
# Hunt's Point

That was all the test I needed. I was ready to go take a slow, long walk out to Hunt's Point, quizzing her phone numbers and getting personal information on how we were going to get this money. When we arrived, I called on all the knowledge that I had learned down in Show World, Peep Land, and the streets. I had no spot, but I was going to make one, slowly walking down the hill toward Seneca and Garrison Avenue.

It was dark and quiet! A little off the main track, I noticed a bush up close to the wall and a little milk crate. I took the crate and put it behind the bush; this would be my headquarters or office. There, from behind the bush, I could watch her and cars, people that pass without being seen. I watched the cars and the interest they showed in her, and I also tried to memorize the car license plates and as much of the person as I could see.

Things went well the first couple of days. Money wasn't too fast, but slow money was better than no money because it was sure money, and it was our money! Some nights, it would be $120 to $150 for six hours of work. She wanted coke, cigs, drinks, and food, so till the next day, that left me with very little money to hustle with. Condoms, carfare. Shit! I was right back where I started.

Usually, she gave me the money after each trick, and this one-time thing was going so well. She caught another date in a white van. Shit, I did not see her for almost three hours. I had almost given up when she came teary-eyed and ruffled.

"What happened," I asked.

"Upon entering the van, there was another guy in the back. They drove off. I was raped! Fucked in the ass, and they took the money," she said.

Nothing hurt or bothered me more than hearing the money was gone! "The money is gone" is all I heard! Now, I had to go into some pimp shit—cold and heartless. "Bitch! I need my money!" I never was physical with women, always mental. "I feel for you," I said, "but I told you never to get in the car with two people. Always check, and if there are two, let one get out. Now what you going to do?"

"Get that money, Daddy," she said.

Well, time is money, money is time, and you're starting to waste both. Now get back out there and get some money, bitch."

She smiled and said, "Ok, Magic."

I was getting tired of this chump change I was getting from her. Plus, it was taking time away from the coke game, which was starting to grow. And Hunt's Point is no joke late at night. Once, two guys were standing on the corner of Seneca and Garrison, smoking and talking a little too long. I had a Walkman in my pants that I let the clip show with my hand covering the rest. I stepped to them, making sure the clip was visible, and looked them straight in the eyes. "Yo, my man, yawl can stand here and talk, but my girl working, and you're making tricks nervous."

Well, they left, but they didn't look happy, for they had never seen where I came from. Ten minutes later, a van driven by the driver looked at me and seemed to be talking to more than one as they drove past me and turned. I quickly walked to the bush and got inside; minutes after sitting on my Dellwood milk crate, they were back; this time, the side door was open with three guys ready to jump out. They looked left and right, but the bush had saved me. I realized it was time to move on and focus on that coke I picked up from Cozy and Fox.

My name was getting known around the block and the bars. Money was stacking, looking good, so good the girl upstairs took me to a hotel twice. Then, she kicked her baby daddy out and moved me in. The sex was good, hot, two pure Scorpio fire which was passionate we were. But I had just gotten out of a relationship and hadn't drunk champagne. She helped me dull the pain of losing my baby momma, and the cocaine did the rest, and what you know, Joan and girlfriend sniffed a little sum tin, sum tin. That became steady weekly.

Then, there were some employees at her job at Banker's Credit and Commerce, an Indian-owned bank with kings and real princesses; she was the bank's president and personal secretary. He always brought her exotic gifts from faraway places, perfume from Paris, and chocolates from Switzerland. I did not mind. I was also doing a lot of shopping. Babydolls and a wig makeup heel—I liked shopping for my girl. I tell her, "Leave all that to me."

On the way over there, I bumped into an old friend from Blackjacks named Peaches. "Hey, Magic," she called.

"Peaches, what's up? Where are you headed?"

"Over to Show World?"

"Oh, yeah, my girl, too. This is her first day." I introduced them to Peaches, saying, "This is Senaca, and Senaca, this is Peaches." Yeah, Peaches was a gorgeous, chocolate, slim veteran in the game. "Well, it's that time, yeah, honey, have a good night." I was off, back uptown, at the spot club, whites pool hall it was called back in the day. I had time to kill, not having to be downtown until two o'clock. I felt good my girl was in an established club, which was classy and secure. The only question I had in my mind was, "How much will she make there?" and I wanted it all. Two came quickly, and I was there early.

"Show World pays a weekly salary," she said. "It goes by how many coins you get at the end of the week. But I made two hundred in tips."

"What? Just for peeps and dancing. Peaches, that girl can dance! Yeah, she's been doing this awhile," I said. "This transvestite has the name Seneca working their magic. Well, she has your name, and you're the real Seneca. Don't worry about that." Shit! Two hundred a night. Without fuckin or sucking. That was damn good. I was impressed, more so when she put it all in my hand and said, "Let's go home."

We hopped in the silver shadow and headed uptown. My standings changed two hundred a day with the coke business flowing. *What can go wrong?* I thought. Well… Joan said, crying, "You don't spend time with me. I want to go to the movies to see Karate Kid, playing up on the Concourse, RKO Theater."

I had a business deal down at the club at nine. At two o'clock, I picked my girl up. Not wanting to hear her mouth, I said, "Ok, let's go." I'd take the product with me. Make the deal after the movie is over; be it about nine, then. Well, we were just about to enter the theater when this guy asked me, "Would you like to buy some shoes?"

"What size?" the guy asked.

"Twelve," I replied.

As I asked to see them, a police car rolled by slowly. The guy wanted $25 for the shoes; they were nice and my size. Wouldn't you know that with over $800 in my pocket, I was trying to haggle with him? I learned a painful lesson that day. When you got it good, don't be cheap…?

Well, the police started to back up. I passed my man a purse containing seven and a half grams of coke, some packaged in aluminum foil in fiftys and twenty-fives, and a couple of ounces of weed in baggies, too. Joan tried to push us toward the ticket booth. She never got the hint. She stayed while the police rode up, and an officer asked, "What's going on here, guys?"

"Nothing, Officer," I said, just looking at some shoes.

"Yeah, it doesn't look like that to me." His focus seemed to be on Joan; she was scared, and it showed on her face. "What's in that bag?" he asked.

"You don't have to answer that," I said.

He shouted, "Shut the fuck up!! Don't tell me what I can't do. Open that bag right now!"

Joan started unzipping the bag slowly, and the plastic began to show, pulling it all the way out. When she did, the cuffs came out, and we were both arrested. I didn't want to start out so early with a drug possession charge since they didn't find drugs on me. I told Joan, "Hold that charge, and we'll be out in the morning." It was a tough night, but we were out in the morning.

When Joan told the police it was hers, you should've heard the police. They were so pissed and said to her, "You taking this charge for this scumbag, piece of shit!"

While they were searching me, they pulled out my money—$1,650. "Hey, Lieutenant, look at the money he's carrying. You're a drug dealer, boy."

No, Officer, I'm not!!"

"Well, what are you doing with so much money."

"We were going shopping," I said.

"With sixteen hundred."

"Yeah, we were buying furniture, having a housewarming party. That's vacation money."

"Yeah, tell it to the judge, lock them up."

Overnight in the precinct, I know, was rough for her, and I was also wondering what the judge was going to say. While entering central booking the next day, I saw her, tatted and sleep-deprived. I smiled and winked at her, indicating that it was going to be alright. As I entered the men's cell, I was shocked. Everyone from the Club was there, Sgt. Tee, Buffalo, all were the big fish, seven all together. I thought I was at the Club. *What the fuck!* I thought.

It seemed the same time I was supposed to be there with the business transaction was to take place. It was raided, and a gun and drugs were found; they arrested all seven beings, and no one knew anything about it. Sargent was making noise, talking about how bullshit the charges were, and they'd all be out by today. "We're the magnificent seven," he boasted.

I wasn't so sure, but one thing I was glad about was that I didn't go there last night. It was fun with all of them, and time went by fast.

"Jimmy Holloway," the guard called, "time to talk to the lawyer."

"What you here for?" he asked.

"Well, you should know. Why you ask me?"

"It says disorderly conduct," the lawyer said. "This is a desk appearance; you should have been released at the precinct."

After appearing before the judge, I was released. I waited for my girl, and she was also released with five years' probation. The other mofos they kept. The magnificent Seven, ha!

"Let's go get some breakfast, then we go see Karate Kid!! I said, and she laughed. What a day! My money was vouched, and I was not going to get my drugs back. But they gave me back my $800. Gotta be more careful; this sensitivity about others must stop when it comes to business and must always come first. Got away this time. Next time, I might not be so lucky. It's payday downtown at Show World. Let's go check the trap. Yes, I was so relieved over the outcome in court. I was also very concerned about my girlfriend, who was hardworking and a mother of two. This meant if something happened to her, I would be responsible. I'm not taking care of no one else's dick anymore. Although I did it before, I'm done.

My last girl already had two kids whom I grew to love when I met her. Then she had one from me. After six years, I was still hurting over the breakup. So, I intended to make more and go farther than I went with her, and she'd regret she threw me out. We had to go around the corner to pick up the check. It was $1,200. Enough to ree up. Now, we must cash it, and most importantly, I must get it. I thought it'd be difficult, but it wasn't. She said two things that blew my mind. The first thing she said, while holding a $1,200 check, "Is this all I can make?"

"Well, are you ready for the big leagues?"

"Yes, I am."

"Well, I know a place where you dance on stage called Paradise. Then, they have private rooms. What goes on there is between you and the date; it all remains private."

"Sounds good. Let's go shopping. There's a leather jacket I want to get for you, and I need outfits so you can have the rest."

"Great decision. I agree, but I make all the decisions; you just put that money in my hand. Now, go cash this check. I'll wait here smoking a cigarette."

I smacked her on that fat ass she had. She went into the bank; it was a good day. I bought her a leather, and then we went to audition at Paradise Theater with bags in our hands; we went and applied for Paradise Theater and upgraded to forty-six and Broadway. She got put on and was ready to start that night.

"Excellent! What time you get off?"

"Two o'clock."

"You need anything?"

"No. Just be here to pick me up."

"No need to worry about that. I'll always be there, so hit 'em in the head, see you at two."

Now I got re-up, money time to check my connect, remembering Fox saying that he'd be at The Recovery Room on the Concourse, a small hidden spot nicely decorated. Yeah, he was there. He told me, "My brother got picked up, so I don't have the weight you need. But how about this?" He pulled out a thirty-two revolver in a threatening way, then laughed, saying, "I was only playing."

Yeah, right! I now needed a new connection. With Cozy, I got a good vibe, and Fox was a little young and reckless. I went back to the Club to play some cards or cee lo until my girl got off, plus I had to score some coke.

At the Club that night, there was an old guy who looked a little like Smokey Robinson and that he'd been around for a while, wavy partied hair, seemed comfortable and known by everyone, sniffing out a bill by the ce-lo table I had seen him before up on Boston Road.

"They don't play nice up there. Hey, what's up? My name's Hank. I was just letting a few checks this good shit out," that guy said.

Vance was behind him and said, "Yeah, it's good."

Well, shit, I was right on time. The stuff he had wasn't as good as mine because he put a cut on it. I never did. So, he and I got to talking. There were a lot of things I didn't know about this game, and he was pulling my coat at a cost to me, but it was a small thing.

My girl downtown was pulling in eight or twelve hundred a night, so he became my connection. I wanted to go directly to his connection, but it didn't matter how much I spent; he was not introducing me to his. So, I never spent the money I wanted, for he was ciphering shit.

I had to deal with it until Cozy got back. Things started to really move: cash, clothes, clubs, jewelry. It had been a couple of months. My girl and I sometimes hung out with Hank and his girl, shooting pool on the spot. Drinks were always on me.

Hank's girl was at least twenty years younger than he was, so she loved hanging out with me and my girl, Seneca, or Joan; well, I never had them together. Guess what? Hank told her what game I was in, and I always caught her staring at me. But I wouldn't disrespect our business relationship, though she seemed to be more woman than he could handle.

Chocolate with huge hips, we enjoyed many nights shooting pool at the club, sniffing, you know, doing the ladies' night thing, my dollar. I quickly got bored with this old-school cat. But before I left, I bought blue steel, .357 Smith & Wesson, from him. His girl was mad that he sold it, but cash money rules any and everything.

Getting it was like a new toy on Christmas. I bought a shoulder holster and a side holster, too. There was nothing more that I wanted from him. Plus, Cozy was back.

The Paradise Theater was paying off big time, and she already set a record at Show World; she was at the top of the food chain there. Daily income. Nine and twelve a night. So many clubs and dancing. Top-shelf drinks. Fine clothes and jewelry.

"What up, my man, Magic?" Cozy Hollered.

I greeted him at the bar at the Recovery Room, "Yo, Cozy. Good to see you."

"Good to be seen. You look like a million."

"Yeah, a little better," I said while pulling on my two-tone red and gray leather jacket.

"You have that thing for me?"

"Yeah, I already hooked it up for you, Magic. Just drop the cash. Fox has the stash."

I followed Fox to the bathroom, and as I went in, I pulled my Three-Fit from my shoulder holster, placed it on his neck, and said, "If you ever pull that little shit thirty-two out on me again, you be eating it."

As he turned around and looked at Smith and Wesson, he said, "Oh, shit, Magic. You not playing."

"Not at all."

I got my shit and was out. Things really started to get good for us, mainly for me. We'd party after work, sniffin' all over the Bronx and Manhattan, Disco Fever, DJ Red Alert from Three Seventy-One, and DJ Hollywood from Roof Top. Within six months, we were all over Red Parrott, Studio Fifty-Four; once, me and my two girls went to Plato's Retreat, fifty for me and twenty-five for the girls. Soon, as the manager saw me, he came to me and said, "Listen, I know what you're doing; it's none of that here; everything is free."

"Oh, no, we only came here for fun with each other."

"Well, ok, let me show you around. Here's your pool-size hot tub, here's the free buffet, private room orgies in those rooms, and here's where you get naked. No one wears clothes beyond this point."

My girls had a ball or two, and they took turns blowing me underwater. Oh, the other girl, she was a prospect trying to get her to join me, so like an interview, I was always looking to expand. Six months into the business, it was growing in clientele. Having interviews all the time, looking to grow this pimp game, coke game, and any and every opportunity that could bring me money. Like, my man, James Brown's song when he sings. Having fun got money to burn. But things were about to change in ways I never expected. Rapidly!

While cruising the hood, playing my jams in the silver shadow. Vanity lights on the side. Two equalizers. CB console. Feeling good on an early Friday night and looking for something to get into. When up ahead, a car stopped, the door opened, and a girl got out. As I pulled up, the driver said, "Yo! You want to drive this girl to Harlem? I'm not going there."

I'm always looking to recruit; I quickly assessed her assets curiously, thinking why he put her out. She was young, light-skinned, and had a small frame, and she had a lazy eye.

"Where you going?" I asked.

"One-Hundred-Fifty-Fifth Street and Amsterdam," she said.

"For what?"

"I'm getting two twenties for me and my twin sister."

"Shit, this your lucky day. I got that right here," I said. I pulled out a plastic baggy.

She said, "No, I need it cooked up, Base Rock."

# Chapter Five
# The Twins

I had no idea Richard Pryor had gotten burned while freebasing last year. "You know how to do it?" I asked.

"Yes, my sister knows."

"Okay, well, I'll take you. If it's good, I'll buy a couple."

"Okay, okay," she said.

Silver Shadow was there with quickness, and this girl was just as fast. I called her Twin One. She was back with the biggest caps, stuffed up to the top. It was overflowing. "Shit, these are the twenties. Get me four of them."

I gave her eighty dollars. She moved so fast it was frightening. I thought she was running off with my money, but just as fast as she left, she returned even faster. We were back across the 155 Street Bridge into the Bronx. To my surprise, she lived down the block from my grandma's house.

So, upstairs I went, excited to try something new and meet the other twin. Their apartment was sparsely furnished with Dellwood milk crates. "This is Magic. He took me there. This is his first time. He brought his own."

"Ah, nice to meet you. I brought one for you. Here. Always take care of the house. I learned that as a rule." She smiled. "Mind if I call you Twin Two?"

"Yes, you can call me Twin One because I'm the oldest."

"You got it."

All the while, she was loading up a glass bowl, and Twin Two was fixing one up on the table. Twin One lit the torch, put the pipe to her mouth, and fire to that rock, and a cloud swirled around the bowl, quickly filling it as she inhaled deeply. Then, she passed it to me and told me to pull as she applied a little fire. I inhaled, and when I exhaled, two years had passed…

The twins' house became my first crack house, with a training and entertainment room in the back, which I used for privacy. It was for those paying freak-out customers and sometimes for me, but that's about business. I was buying very little cocaine, only to cook up from Harlem, breaking it down, then redistributing it, making some of my money back.

I now had many connections all over Harlem. I became my best customer. Hotels and motels, the fliest of girls. Crack houses all over Harlem: Red Door, Silver Door, Black Door. Man, the nights were abuzz with crack! They had twenty bowls and torches, numbered, with girls cleaning the bowls, refilling the torches, and trading the residue they got from cleaning the bowls for the white rock.

I was learning every night about the power of this drug over me and others. It became a tool I used to manipulate and devastate my prey. It seemed to give me energy, motivation, and sexual urges that were hard to control. Once I took a puff, I wanted my dick sucked. I spent so many nights riding around freebasing in the car, carrying a bowl everywhere.

At the club one night, I sat down at the poker game. All the usual players were there with their dollar bills filled with coke, talking shit, drinking. While I was receiving my cards, I was loading up my bowl and igniting my torch, engaging the fire to the bowl, and blasting off. They all looked at me strangely.

"What the fuck is that?" Buffalo asked.

Sgt. and the rest looked in amazement. While exhaling, I said, "Base rock! Y'all sniff. I smoke it."

"I don't want to see that shit here," Sgt. said. "Do that shit in the back."

Okay, Buffalo came. He was curious and became my customer. In the months to come, cracks exploded in the Bronx. There were crack houses all over the Bronx, and I was an elite member, well, at least up in the Bronx, and used them for trading. The women there said that when I came here with a trick or treat, they would get a cut, and we ate all night. Oh, no, they were never satisfied. They wanted to smoke like me. Most preferred to suck my dick without a condom all night for the crumb I would give them. Then, work with a condom for less time and more money. Then, you can get your own.

Now, the added energy that freebasing gave me had me up for some time, but not more than two days, and then rested for a whole day. The money that I made in the streets was nothing compared to what I was getting downtown on a daily basis. I guess being so busy flying around basing, I didn't pay much attention when the money was short or when she was sick and things were slow. She almost broke the record at Show World—missed it by only two coins.

Then, one night, I came to pick her up while waiting at Howard Johnson, having turkey and mashed potatoes. Seneca walked in a little after two a.m. "It's really slow, Daddy. I didn't make any money."

"What? How could that be? You're the baddest bitch up there! Well, you made enough to pay for this meal."

"No."

"What? Let's go." I dropped a twenty and walked out. "We're going to get to the bottom of this shit really quick."

She came clean with very little pressure; we don't lie to each other. Well, not to me. Come to find out the manager, Nancy, that fat white bitch, was selling rock upstairs. She and Peaches and a few others. So, no wonder my money was funny. But in Nancy's Fancy. I found Nancy a hotel room on the twenty-third on the Eastside. She was startled to see me. "How did you find out where I stay?" she asked.

"Don't worry about it. I know your house in Connecticut. Don't sell it or give my girl anything, or you will see me up there. But if it wasn't for her, it would be someone else my girl was hooked on."

She started disappearing for days, then weeks. Money started getting tight for me, too; I was hooked. On the days that I saw her after the runs she'd been on, there were also significant changes in me. I moved my grandma uptown with my aunt; now it's time to get down and dirty.

"Baby, look, if you want to get high, get high with me, or here are some of my spots where you can go. You don't have to anymore. Ok?"

"Ok."

So, I took her up to meet the twins; they loved her. Not everyone! One bitch I had to slap for wanting to fight my girl. I told her to stop and that I wouldn't let my girl fight her. I did fuck her before, but Pow! "Sit your ass down, I told you she's not fighting."

My girl geeks out when she gets high, paranoid, can't talk, scary ass. Once, while smoking, I said, "Pass the bowl."

She was like, "Mmm!"

I said, "Let it go."

She said, "It's holding me."

So now, after she gets off, she wants to smoke all night long, missing work. If I don't give her money, she'll make her own. It is not going to work; money flows slowly. Joan was crying once again. Someone told her they saw me driving with three girls in the car, plus, once again, I wasn't spending enough time with her. I was becoming overwhelmed, coping with the drug distribution, carrying a gun, pressure, and paranoia. Good, sound, and wholesome reality were out; I was caught up in the game now.

Joan was holding me back. Before I could tell her, she threw all my clothes out: silk, cashmere, and leather bomber. Shit, I didn't care. Seneca was very happy; she thought she'd have more time with me. Well, I didn't like it. But we were hooked on this new drug that was exploding all over the City of New York.

I had several spots all over the Bronx where I supplied drugs and tricks. The twins' house was getting a lot of attention now. Customers were coming; once, a well-known rapper came through, wanted a private room, made a purchase, and two girls ran to him with their bowls into the backroom. Twin One saw how much money I was getting and wanted more than I gave her. Plus, when I didn't have it, she would have others sell up there, and after they smoked up any tricks money, they were allowed to sleep there. Wanting me to throw them out, which was more work I didn't need.

With Grandma gone, well away with my aunt, I turned it up, out trolling the streets looking for prospects. Bring them to the Magic Show; there, they go through intense training, loyalty, willingness, and the ability to focus on getting money, not getting high. Most are so willing while the rock is there, but when it's gone, so are they. Go out, get one trick for twenty dollars, then want to come back with that chicken scratch they spent two hours to get. I tried to step them up. Don't get high while working. And most importantly, only at the house! Magic House of Pleasure.

Sometimes, I have four women there, one more knocking on the door. "Come on in, you're just in time. We're having a 'who sucks the best dick' game. Want to play?"

"Sure, but not in front of them."

"Shit, we were all having fun together before you came interrupting. Now you want to change the rules. Get out of here; you're wasting my time."

"Ok, wait. I'll do it! Give me a blast first."

Well, after I gave her a blast, she was so paranoid that her dick-sucking skills went out the window. This is what I explained to the women that were there, "Get the money first, then get high after, only get high here, where I supply the drugs."

Seneca was happy. Now, she had a place where she could get high on her own. And no one was going to tax her. Was this a good idea? Well, I no longer had to worry about her coming home and scrounging the city to find her. Money wasn't flowing strong, for I now had to include her and me. We smoked for two days and rested for two days when we broke.

Now, times when the downtown money ran out, we'd go to Hunts Point, Seneca Ave. She was seasoned now in the game, at the top of the food chain. Instead of a crate, it was the Silver Shadow parked on Seneca Ave and Garrison Ave. Now they know me on the set, that's Pimp Magic's spot.

Shit, I didn't have to go there; I just sent my girls there, and they came back with the dough. So, they were happy, not me.

My girl, Seneca, didn't get along with too many girls. But when I found Crissy, a white girl, she somewhat liked her, and I did, too. Crissy was high energy, and she catered to the Caucasian persuasion, also blacks; anyway, she knew how to get money with very little inspiration from me. She worked the west side, eleven and tenth. She heard a lot about Hunts Point and wanted to go. So, one summer evening, we went—the four of us—Seneca, Crissy, Silver Shadow, and me.

After I let the girls out, I drove around doing the math, checking out the set, mainly letting the set check me out, not hearing the whispers, "That's Magic." Letting all pimps and hoes know I'm on the set with a new white girl; most pimps I didn't know or care to know, but the hoes and crackheads knew. "That's Pimp Magic, carrying a .357." Yeah, I let them tell it.

After a couple of hours, I went back to check my trap. As I was pulling up, what did I see? They're laughing, talking while eating pizza, tricks passing by. So, now I put my pimp hat on. "What the fuck is this, lunchtime? Did I say it's a fuckin' lunch date?" Then, I slapped the pizza out of Seneca's hand, and Crissy threw hers away. "Get the fuck back to work," I said, "and eat when it's time to eat. Where's my money? Hope you ain't spent it all on food. Baby, you know better; this is no place to be sleeping. Oh, six hundred. I'm kind of hungry; let's go get something to eat."

"Now that you're here, Crissy, you can come out here on your own or together." And she did.

One afternoon, she left in the morning. I hear screaming in the hallway. "Magic! Magic! Open the door, open the door." As soon as I opened the door, she ran in.

Behind her, a big-ass white boy ran toward the door. "She got my money," he said.

"Wait a minute, back up. She lives here; let me hear her story. Crissy, what's up?"

"He gave me a hundred and said he just wants to talk. That all?

"Okay. Yo, my man, she says you gave her a hundred just to talk."

"Yeah, I did, with a beer."

"Well, we don't have beer here, but you go get some and come back and talk; she'll be here. That hundred dollars is hers to keep. Copy!"

When he came back with beer, we all sat, drank, and talked; I even left them alone for a spell. When about an hour elapsed, I came out, pointed at my watch, and gestured, "Wrap it up." He was gone.

"Crissy, I will admit, that was fast, and that's good, whether it's downtown or out of town. But here in Magic Town, we fuck and suck with a condom always. Sure, if you can get the cash quickly without doing anything. That's something else, and we don't do that here in my home without me expecting what goes down."

While I was talking, Seneca came with another white trick, walking into the building. "That's my man," I heard her say. He walked toward me, extending his hand and saying, "You must be Magic."

"Yes, that's my name. Your girl, Seneca, told me about you. I tried getting her to come with me to a hotel, and she said this is the only place she smokes at, and you are cool with it."

"That's true," I said. "Well, here's a hundred. I guess I won't see you no more," he said.

"Oh, please, that's chicken scratch." I pulled out a fatter bankroll. "Believe me, there's no need for me to run out. I want you to come back. You want another girl?"

"Yeah, sure, you can do that?"

"For sure, go on in. I'll be back in a couple of minutes. Magic House up and running."

But this trick, after he spent over five hundred, he asked if I could use an AK-47. He wanted to sell it for more cracks.

I said, "Sure."

He said, "I'll be back."

Cause you can't stay here without money, I thought to myself.

He was Italian, and in less than two hours, he was back with the AK-47 and a fragmentation grenade. I was an expert in weapons and grenades in the army. But I wasn't an arms dealer. And this guy, thirsty, wanted me to sell shit so he could get high. Pimping me. I'm not walking around with an AK-47.

Trying to sell it, but I took the grenade to the Jamaicans down the block and spoke, "Yo, man, I got a grenade to sell you, brother."

"What?!" he said.

"Yes, brethren, a fragmentation grenade. What am I supposed to do with that?"

"Well, dem Dominicans are growing strong up the block. They might want to move on you."

"Me not worry about that!! Where is it?"

"Right here in this potato chip bag." I pulled it out.

"Oh, shit! How much?"

"Give me a hundred and some weed, and I got an AK-47. Everything for five."

"Well, I got four. To tell the trick, I got three." I gave him one fifty and signed the girls on him. When he was breaking, the party stopped, and the shop closed. We need our rest.

Two, no more than three days of rest, then we have to feed the beast, and it is hungry! As much as I tried, I couldn't put the genie back in the bottle. As for my girls, they didn't have any reason to stop. It started to get hectic carrying the gun, picking up the drugs, breaking it up, and dealing with these women's problems. The money wasn't coming in, well, it was coming in; it's that we were smoking it up. Fifteen hundred and better every night—hotels and motels, two women, shit, three, wait! Wait, take it easy. Yes, it's so easy to swing the mantra with drugs and money. But when the drugs and money go, so goes the fantasy.

The twins' spot got taken over by thugs supported by the Dominican. Drug spots were turning up rapidly all over the Bronx. People were looking for places to smoke with bowls and torches. I knew them all who had the best head, clean women, and dirty, safe, for a price. Had to cut off the relationship with the twins. Between the thug and the Dominican copying what I started there, their supply was strong, so they flourished. The place got hot with the traffic all night, all day. Shit, sometimes, I was a customer.

One night, I came through, and the girls were happy to see me. They wanted me to entice a girl to come out of the room because she had money and drugs and was spending it all with three dudes. I had inhaled a big blast of icy rock from Harlem, exhaled, and said, "Why should I stop her show? She's having fun with them, and they with her. What, y'all mad she's not smoking with y'all? I know if I was spending money with three women, I'd be. Plus, I'm not a bouncer, not my spot."

"Yo, fuck it! Where's my half?" Twin One said.

I took a razor blade and separated four rocks; I took one for myself and gave the rest to Twin One and Twin Two. The other girl was Barbie Ann, a real cutie pie I had my eyes on for a minute. I knew she sniffed, but freebase. She was so sexy at all times, having Bette Davis's eyes. I got to add her to my stable. And did, but she was trouble; there were problems with the other two girls I had. I decided to still give her a key, and in less than three days, I took it back on the strength of Seneca and Crissy, saying she never had any money and she was lazy!

When I took the key from her, she had tears in her eyes. Bye! Time for pretty petty.

The next day, I ran into Bear and his wingman.

"Yo, Magic. I heard Bobbi's up in your stable now!! I know she's making money; we trained her," Bear exclaimed, telling him about the hundred thousand dollars we had.

"What do you mean? Ya'll had a hundred thousand and look the way you look? I wouldn't tell that to too many people. But I put that hoe out in less than three days. My girls said she brings in twenty, thirty dollars then crumb off hundreds of our shit."

At that time, Twin Two walked up. Twin One said, "You know how I do." She smiled and shook her head a couple of times.

"Shit, if you see her, tell her that Magic's House isn't cheap. There's a certain standard I want to impose on the women, although we're base heads later."

I peeled off. "Oh, I didn't tell you I brought a Chrysler New Yorker, four forty engines like a living room. Cruising, checking the spots and streets, looking for tricks and hoes to be."

On this day, I saw an old friend from Bryant Avenue. Well, he wasn't all that a friend, more so a nemesis. Some fifteen years ago, I stuck him twice on the schoolyard basketball court in front of everybody.

"Well, I see he's a little buffed," I wasn't at all intimidated. I honked the horn and called out, "Yo, Butch, what's happening, man?"

"Hey, Jimmy, what's happening, man? I just got out of jail."

"How long?" I asked.

"Eight," he said.

"You know where to get some crack?" he asked.

"You got dough. I know where to go; it's fat twenties and dimes. I was going there right now. Get in." He looked like he was getting high earlier, but that was not my business.

The spot was on Sherman Avenue, 165 Street. He went in with me. I copped six; it was still early. "You this my man, he's cool," and I stepped away from the door. Butch stepped to the peephole; I think he brought two.

"They fat, right?" Yeah.

"Well, you're good. I have some things to take care of."

"Yeah, I'm good," he said. I had a spot upstairs I didn't tell him about; as I said, we weren't all that tight, and buying two wasn't enough for me to show him. Magic House has to be fed and get them ready for work.

Seneca was excited when I arrived; Crissy was too, but she never showed it in front of Seneca. We sat at the table and opened all six caps on the mirror, and with the razor blade, I divvied out three hits. We loaded up our stems, and all took a blast. After this, we got ready for work. Did you notice I said stems, no longer using bowls or torches? Yes, times were changing.

Well, the girl's gone to work. I went to play some cards or cee-lo at the spot and hit a little something at the bar, which was my usual routine. That night, I ran into my old friend OB.

"What's up Jimmy, long time no see," OB said, a childhood friend I went to school with. He was always little and brought a lot of candy to school. He always gave me some for protection from the cliques in school. Now, he was running a dope ring in Co-Op City.

"What you been up to, Jimmy?"

"I've been keeping a little coke while I got three hoes working, Midtown and Hunts Point, doin' alright."

"But who's running with you?" he asked.

"Shit, me, Smith and Wesson; they got my back," I said, pulling my jacket back and exposing the shoulder holster.

"Well, an army of ants can eat up an elephant. See, I'm little, but I roll deep."

"Like buying protection?"

"No, like commanding protection. I'll take a look into that. My experience is it's safer to be by yourself. You don't have to split with anyone, and if shit goes down, you're not going to rat on yourself. Time to go, good seeing you."

Time to make a few runs, pick up some rock and check on the spot over on Sherman Avenue. This time, I was going upstairs to the third floor. Right after copping my shit, coming in behind me was Butch; he was also copping, looking a little ravaged like he'd been out since I saw him almost two days ago.

"Yo Jimmy, where you goin'?"

"Upstairs, I'll be back." Whew, I was glad the elevator door was closing. Although he was getting his own, I didn't want to talk.

Upstairs, Kiki's house was always clean, and they respected and loved some Magic. "Where you been?" she asked.

"You're looking good," I said as I sat down at the table, looking around at the people that were there, thinking, who was going to suck this dick when I took this hit.

I was just getting comfortable when someone knocked on the door. Kiki got up to answer it.

"It's a girl, Magic."

"Tell her to come in."

"She doesn't want to," she said. "Come out."

"Okay," I said and went to the door. There was a young, slim girl, nicer than the girl Kiki had there. "What's up? Why can't you come in?" I asked.

"I don't get along with Kiki."

"So, what's up?" I said while putting my hand between her legs.

Before she could answer, Butch walked up. "Yo, Jimmy, you're going to look out."

"Yo, Butch, what's up? I got you."

As I thought about what to give him, I saw this dude who I didn't know. I spurned around toward him and said, "What I got for you!! I don't even know you. Butch, that's your man."

"Yeah, he alright. You better school him."

While I was looking at him, Butch jumped behind me, arms around my neck. Off guard, I tried to pull his arm off and kick his man, whom I saw coming toward me. But before I could do anything, I blacked out. Then, I guess he threw me down the stairs. I felt someone going through my pockets and then screaming.

"Oh, my God, Magic. Somebody, call an ambulance!"

"Oh, my God, Magic! You alright?"

"Yes, I'm alright. You see my keys?"

"Yes."

"My car is parked out front. Watch it."

"Okay, don't worry, the ambulance is on the way. You'll be okay."

I blacked out after that and dreamed about Butch and what I should have done years ago when I had the chance to kick his ass. I let my guard down and thought we were friends. A costly mistake in this game could mean your life. It pained me more to think about letting this sucker-ass nigger get the best of me. I thought about what I was going to do to him when I saw him.

My girls were in shock; they couldn't believe anyone could take me down. Well, here's a painful lesson well learned. And what OB had told me: "An army of ants will eat up an elephant." I took to heart what OB had said and went about recruiting a crew. The first was Troop, followed by Jeff and Poogie. Poogie had a thirty-eight short nose. He gave it to me to look at after he took the bullets out. I liked that. I never liked working with others because I had to feed them. But I thought of ways that would help them earn their keep. And I was not very patient, but for security, I'd try it.

Now, along with the girls, I got these guys to school and motivated them. Troop was short and light-skinned, had hazel eyes, and was well-built with a wingspan like Bruce Lee. We worked out together while talking gangster shit. Isometrics pull-ups were a good way to bond; my trust was a different thing.

"But if you want to eat here, I need loyalty and respect," I emphasized.

"Yo, Magic, I got my own way of making money. Shit, I might help you step up your game," Troop said while working out.

"Okay, sounds good!! Show me. Talk is cheap. I'm pulling a G a night, and then I got to feed my family," I replied.

"Stop crying, Magic. You're getting plenty of money."

"This is the kind of shit I don't like. You can't eat off mine. This ain't no fifty-fifty shit, motherfucker. Don't get it twisted," I asserted. "Let's leave it there.

A couple of hours later, there was a knock on the door. "It's Troop, yo, Magic, open up!! Just robbed the numbers, man.

"Who? Beasley? The old guy with glasses? Yeah, I know him," I said.

"Well, I don't. Here's six hundred. Break me off a little something."

"Oh, what the fuck? " I said, and we both laughed. He stayed for a few hours and left under the cover of darkness.

Troop never touched the pipes; he'd roll what he called a "dinky dong," trying to get me to, but I took too much time. A lot of robberies were going on in the area. When asked, I knew nothing.

The crack epidemic was exploding with the help of Dominicans buying apartments from crackheads, taking and selling from there, and hiring workers, lookouts, and dealers. That's where I met Jeff. He started out as a lookout for them.

He had a little habit, too, like smoking whoolers, and he was young, around nineteen.

I let him smoke his whoolers in my house during his breaks, and he'd be breaking and tapping bags. When he was short, I gave him money to make up the count while asking many questions about the workings of the business and instilling the idea of making money off our people and not putting anything back.

The one who ran things was named Ali, strange for a Dominican, but he was the supplier. The second in command was Gordo, which means fat; now, that's a Spanish name. Delivery time, pickup time. They had a few spots around and were starting to expand. I decided I'd let them know I was about girls and that I'd spend some money and had plenty. Maybe we could do business.

After attaining the necessary information from the inside from Jeff and Poogie, we began setting them up for robbery on a regular basis. I didn't like the way Ali was using the community for the drug game, making money, and disrespecting the women and people. My block, my people.

So, when the shipment came in, we told them it was hot; we were undercover and watching. So, they stashed it; we came around quickly and picked it up. We told them we'd call the cops to the building, saying that they found the stash and gave them a little cash. I told them to give Ali some cash, saying we dropped the package. We kept the bulk.

All this was planned in Magic's house, where we divided the spoils while getting high. They smoked whoolers; there were pounds of White Owls and debris everywhere. The twins were also hitting them. Ali was taking a loss on a daily basis and was looking for a new spot.

Well, my idea was to rent out my house for two hundred a week, starting with a thousand upfront for the first month. I could sell crack from twelve in the afternoon till two AM. My room was in the back, and I wanted to come and go anytime and bring whoever I wanted. They understood my offer, and we shook hands.

That week, they came and secured the door with wood from the door to the floor and gave me five hundred and a thousand worth of drugs for the first month's rent. Let the party begin! And money roll. When two o'clock came, they left. Then, if any customers came after two, I sold them the same color caps throughout the night. And they were coming!! Never did I let them see me smoking; they tend to disrespect you when they know.

The first two weeks went fast; people knew I had Ali's shit. The twins found out about the deal. Twin One said that Ali was not going to pay me my money one way or the other. Sure enough, at the end of the first month, Ali denied paying me, citing the door he had put in and that he was not making much money there. I let two weeks go by, and I still got no payments. Well, while playing the game with them, I'd been weighing the possibility and came up with a plan. So, I told my girls not to come around for a while because some shit was about to jump off.

The plan was to use them to establish this place as the top money-making spot in the Bronx, using their drugs and eventually putting them out. And it was time to make it happen.

I called the crack hotline and told them that I rented a room out to a Dominican man; he brought other people and started selling drugs while I was gone. I told them, "I don't like that 'cause I don't do that." My room was in the back, and you'd not find any drugs or paraphernalia there. The plot was set. I told my girls not to come by for a couple of days. However, that was like telling Seneca to come. For that night when I told her, the next day she woke me up in the afternoon with a turkey and parmesan cheese hero. I said, "Seneca. Baby, I said, 'Don't come over for a while.'"

"You don't listen. If someone wants to find me, all they have to do is follow you."

"Well, honey, I'm on my way to work, and I thought you'd be hungry. So, I'll see you tonight."

Strange kind of love, this hustle game, but in this game, we must win.

I let those idiots know to let my girl in when I was in or not, and they were trying to question her devotion to me and wonder why she didn't talk to them. Then they asked,

"Magic, how do you just lay back, and these girls just bring money to you?"

"Well, if I was putting this dick in you, you'll be bringing money too." They all laughed.

I went back into the room and closed the door after finishing the sandwich. I must have fallen asleep, only to wake up to wall-shaking thuds and shouts. "Open up, it's the police! BAM, BAM, BAM! Open the door."

My plan was to jump out the back window onto a truck and go away through the backyard, but while they were still banging, trying to get in, I heard the police. "We got them down here," before two of them jumped out the front fire escape.

"Wait, wait, I'M GONNA OPEN THE DOOR." I slid the four-by-six, opening the door. They burst in, knocking me to the floor, and began kicking the shit out of my ass. "Wait, wait. I'm the one who opened the door." I protested.

"You didn't open it up fast enough," they said and kicked me some more.

I was brought out in handcuffs, no shirt, and neighbors pointing, "Oh, shit, they got Magic."

Shit, I'm glad my girl brought me that sandwich. It was going to be a long night in court. They charged me with the possession of narcotics, one handgun, resisting arrest, and a hundred thousand bail. The next court date was one week later. Would you know if the others were bailed out? Still a little dazed, I arrived at Rikers Island for the first time, Ann Cross Detention. I stayed there for two weeks, and then I was taken to the court, where I spoke with my lawyer. He told me how much time I could face and what they found.

"I don't care about what they found. It's not mine. I'm the one who called the crack hotline and made a report. It should be on file, telling them I don't use drugs, and none will be found in my room. Get the tape. It's on file. I'm sure I made sure of that."

"Well, if it's there, you'll be out next week."

"Next week? Why not now?" I demanded.

"Well, I have many other things I must do, but I'll be getting back to you. So, I guess you will plead not guilty."

"Hell, yeah!!"

The next day, I was out. My apartment was torn the fuck up, I mean destroyed. My little family had a meeting and welcome-back party that night. Seneca, Jeff, Poogie, Troop, most loyal. Topic: Get back, payback. During my time in the lockup, my house was torn up, and the car was towed. I was greeted and treated throughout the night; the morning was better—a chance to exact my compensation.

Ali and his goons showed up; mine were there from last night. Ready to put some closure on this arrangement, one of the main topics throughout the night. What Ali proposed was better than my plan. He wanted to put me in charge, give me a huge number of drugs, and be back in the morning.

As soon as he put the package in my hand and walked away, I looked at Jeff and Troop and said, "I'm out."

I gave a decent amount to each, grabbed my girl, and was a ghost for a while. I went down to Alphabet City in the Village, lying low for a while, coming uptown under the cover of darkness. Once I was spotted, I saw them at the same time they saw me. They weren't going to run up like that; it might have got loud. Well, it was time to blow this place.

I rented a fully furnished room in the Belvedere Hotel on Seventy-Seven and Broadway—a step-up closer to work and the big money. Got into a nice routine, Big Nick Burger Joint downstairs, and they delivered. Cable television that wasn't up in the Bronx yet. Leaving the Bronx was good; it was a new outlook. But the drug habits came too, only stronger. Although we were making money, it was going to drugs, and this wasn't part of the plan. Twelve hundred a night wasn't enough for the two of us. It began a living to use and using to live the way of life.

I was always trying to let the drug make money, keeping me alert. In the corner store down from the hotel, they had a poker machine and slot. I used to tape some thread to a quarter and jingle it ever so lightly until it hit that lever for credit. It'd spin the amount wildly; then I'd go and collect that amount. The store workers liked me; they thought I was lucky. I'd always say, "Not luck, Magic."

One day, in the early afternoon, they were busy because they didn't turn on the machine. I knew how to signal; I was turning it on. Once back there, I noticed a jacket quickly hitting the pockets. I noticed a certain sound, reached in, and pulled out a handful of money, and my heart started pumping wildly. The other pocket had paper; it could have been money orders. I knew there was not much time, so I flipped the switch, went back to the machine, and played a couple of games, and they were still busy.

I walked out the door calmly; as I walked out, I hailed one of those yellow cabs. "Bronx, Third Avenue, 166," I stated, counting on the way up. I got tired after reaching two thousand, and there was still over half left. "Yo, driver, step on it, drive like you're in a rush, 'cause I gotta shit really bad. Here's an extra twenty."

Hotels, motels, crack spots, clubs, gators, silk, dick being sucked in the Silver Shadow, everywhere and anywhere, it was fun and exciting for a while. But a few nights of waking up broke, and my dick raw was a bad feeling. Plus, I didn't even cum. Really, I didn't want to. It was more about the orgasm in my mind; just having your dick sucked is not cheating. Only if you cum? And if I happen to put my dick in the pussy, shit, I will be at the clinic in the morning. Pimping's such a dirty game, and the crack was making it dirtier.

I was back up in the Bronx after a time-out. I heard Al was dead… fell out, some said. Others said a silencer, one to the head, broad daylight. *Such is the fate of most drug dealers,* I thought to myself. Anyway, Magic House was back in business. I sometimes wonder why the landlord never pressed me for the rent. Maybe the AK residue.

Seneca was uptown in a yellow cab, with a hundred-dollar bundle from Eighth Ave, and smoking all the way from Forty-Second and Eighth. Can't stop that. She handed over eight and better. Once she came up on a motorcycle, she had eleven hundred. Her first words were, "You have any now?"

"Sure, I do." That was about the length of the conversation. After she hit that stem, all reality disappeared.

Trying to get her to sleep after she took that first hit was impossible for me, too. She said, "Leave me two hundred; I'm going to this spot or that, then I'm going home." But that never happened.

Once, I told her not to go back down to work because she was getting too high; I had someone else working there, and I didn't want no problems, and she was doing well, then I pulled out a wad of cash—actually newspaper and tore the size of dollars with a twenty on top rubber bands around it.

"Who's working there? Not in my spot; I'm going there now," she said and walked out.

Shit, I was glad money was coming in; after that twenty on the fake roll, I had about forty-six dollars in my pocket. Player pimp one on one, always keep a stash to flash. I think I'll play some poker until two.

Tonight was a good night, heading downtown to pick up my girl. I liked slowly cruising down Broadway, sometimes stopping in Tin Pan Alley to have a drink and a little pool and a bite to eat. I was at the top of my game now, yet lonely in this game. There was no one to trust.

I tried hanging out with Israel; his father, Big Bill, owned the club. The rumor had it that his brother robbed a bank back in the day and bought a couple of private houses and some land. So, Israel was arrogant and self-centered, very disrespectful to his father, who gave him everything.

I admit I was jealous, for no one gave me anything. We hung out and went skating on the Harlem rink rooftop, as well as Skate Fever and the Roxy. He was always competing against me and couldn't beat me at anything. He brought a pair of Jordans and thought he could beat me in ball, then pool, but he had no luck competing against me.

He imitated being a Scorpio to impress the women, but he was a Capricorn. I disliked it, but we hung out a little when I had time. Most people were jealous because I was so handsome and modest. He always wanted to compete with me, and I beat him in everything but chess. That game was new to me, yet I was interested. He liked beating me, laughing, and talking shit, but I kicked his college ass in the pool and talked just as much shit.

One thing about him was that he always wanted to be quicker, faster, stronger, and smarter. He was much on my mind, but I always wanted to hang with him, my nemesis.

We used to pick up abandoned cars; I wiped the police chalk off the door, and he backed up his flatbed truck. We hauled it to Jersey for scrap metal. We made a little something.

We went down to the Roxy; this was when I had gotten kicked out of my baby momma's house. His father helped me and allowed me to stay at the club when I had nothing. Now, he sees me dressing fly, pockets full of money. I admit, I loved flaunting it in his face when he was greasy.

I pulled out a roll and said, "Let's go to the Roxy?"

"Nah," he said, "gotta get up in the morning."

"But I got time to play some chess," I suggested puffin' on some lambsbread.

It's beginning to be a lonely game getting all this money and not being able to trust anyone to understand or share an interest in growing this business. Most were jealous of me anyway; others weren't happy about the drug use and the way I was getting this money.

Most didn't respect it. And I started to disrespect it, too. Pimping was something I thought would get me to the top quickly, but not without a cost. The drugs were never added to the equation, and like an epidemic, it was spreading rapidly.

People were bringing Christmas toys, selling anything, doing anything. Everyone wasn't a drug user, but it affected everyone. The families that were just overcoming the effects of alcohol and the dope era were now devastated by this soul-snatching drug.

The money I was getting from downtown wasn't sufficient for two days. One thirsty morning, I thought to pawn some jewelry to continue my run.

I stopped into a jewelry store with a sign saying, "We Buy Gold." He had just opened it, bringing the jewelry from the safe to put in the window for display. Behind the bulletproof glass, he laid a keyring full of about thirty chains in the daily newspaper.

My mind quickly raced, and I directed him to the well, away from the one by the paper. I had three skinny chains and one gold onyx ring. "Here we go. Good morning. I see the sign saying you buy gold. I'd like to see how much I can get for this," I said, handing him one of the chains.

He took turns scratching it on a stone, then putting acid on it, and then weighing it. While he was busy doing that, I stuck my hand through the well, got my hand on the newspaper, and began pulling and shaking it. The chains on top of it were moving with each shake.

He turned around and said, "I'll give you thirty."

"Thirty?" I pondered.

"Here's a ring and another chain." I offered him, believing that it'd give me enough time.

As soon as he turned around, I was back pulling and shaking the chains, rolling. Finally, one came into the well. I began pulling it out and stuffing it in my pocket like spaghetti.

As he was just turning around, my heart was beating so fast and hard. He said, "I'll give you one seventy."

"Well, give me the ring back and the cash for the two chains. Ring on, cash in hand. Thank you. Can you buzz that door, please," I requested.

He did, and I was out.

Oh, boy, this was huge—thirty or more gold chains, fat and skinny, all real. My mother, auntie, grandma, and my girls—all got chains. I kept a big Cuban link for myself.

I let some friends with identification pawn them for me and gave them money each time they did. I didn't want my face on camera; they might have pictures of me trying to sell it and compare it. Cover your tracks and leave little evidence.

Seneca wanted one for her mother and grandmother. I said, "Okay." Just love those ladies.

I remember one time the mother was hiding in the closet and jumped out when we came in, shouting, "Aa ha! I knew you were still seeing him. What? He got gold on his dick or something? Get the fuck out, you piece of shit!"

Oh, I was startled. In the closet... well, I could accept their feelings; turning their daughter out, I accepted that. But the crack, not me. I thought she should be happy I was bringing her home for some rest. Although we both were using, there still remained a great love between us."

Once, I sincerely prayed to God: "God, I know when Seneca gets off from work, she's going to pick up a package. We are going to use. Lord, I want you to give me the strength to not go out and use after what she brings is finished."

I explained my plan to her and what I wanted to do. I said, "In the morning, we wake up with money and do something nice."

She agreed, saying, "I'll share with you equally the package I'll bring." However, that shit didn't work for her or me. She suggested giving her two hundred of the money that she made, and she was going uptown.

I did, but when she left via cab, I couldn't sleep, worrying about her. Also, I was high and wanted more. This drug was so powerful that once you take it, one hit, forget it—you're going on a rollercoaster ride. So, I strapped myself in and headed uptown, prepared for an all-night ride.

I guess the prayer didn't work. This will be a fight that I will continue to fight; strength will come later...

Although I was a pimp, I didn't tell many people that. They assumed that from the way I dressed and how good I looked, but I didn't hustle in my hood or with people I knew. I tried to appear respectable. I got a girl, but they still wanted me.

One night, standing outside the bar, this girl, Mia, approached me. I knew her and her mother from the block around my sister's age. She asked, "Jimmy, you get high, right?." She probably found out from my sisters because both of them were smoking like mad Russians, and she knew them.

"Now, I'm just saying, I'm selling. That's my work around the corner. You wanna work with me?" she said to me.

I smiled at this young girl who wanted to put me to work.

"Nah, Mia, I don't sell drugs. I get my money a little smoother. Here's twenty; let me see what you got."

"Well, also, I know a spot we can rob."

"What?"

"Yeah, you can put your gun in my bag; they're not going to search me. Then, I give it to you; there's drugs and money."

"Listen, Mia. I'm a pimp; pimps not working that robbery shit; ain't trying to go to jail. But be careful out here." I gave her a hug, and she slipped me twenty pieces. So, that's why she's wearing some gold pieces and designer bags. She always kept herself together. I had more interest in her mother than her, for I believe that was where the money was."

Talking about mothers, my mother's birthday was coming in two weeks. She'd be making forty-eight years young. She was fifteen years older than me. She was more like a big sister to me than a mother. I still love her so much.

Things were getting rough out there, actually grimy. I had to adjust my game, but it still wasn't easy. A good friend, Terry, every time he saw me, he ran to my car trying to sell me crap because he wanted to use it.

I told him, "That's crap," and gave him a cap or two; he ran back to the building with no shoelace while pulling out his stem. Seeing good people and friends and family being controlled by this drug, making them lie and steal their hearts and souls and self-esteem, losing all value of life, including myself.

Looking to make something out of what I had so I could keep smoking. So, I kept a few beats in my pocket, just in case someone who owed me or some stranger out-of-towner presented itself, and it did.

The desire to have my dick sucked was just as strong as the desire to use it; they go together—can't have one without the other. Bliss having both at the same time. Good rocks and heads are hard to find, and I traveled east and west for the best. Sometimes, you get beat by the rock; other times, it beats you for the head. This means that they smoked up hundreds of dollars before you find out the head ain't no good or put a rubber on it first. I don't do anything without a rubber.

"Well, I'm not having my dick sucked without a rubber, ever! Don't waste my time and money, bitch."

One night cruising, I saw the waisted-time bitch. She said, "Magic, can you sell me a twenty? All I got is ten." The nerve of her to ask me for anything as much as she owed. When you live with grime, you must get grimy.

"Yeah, I got you," I said, reaching for the beat bottles. I gave her two in her hand. She took off running with the breadcrumbs down the block so fast; I couldn't believe she could run so fast. I laughed so hard every time I thought about it. And would you believe later at the spot, she wanted to tell people there, "You know, Magic sold me some breadcrumbs."

Bitches tell the whole story of how you ran with it without paying greedy ass bitch plus you owe. People were getting grimy. So was I. I even started dressing down. I saw an old crackhead girl named Speedy, who had just got out from jail, looking the best I had ever seen. It must've been about two years.

"Oh! Look at Magic. I used to drool over him," she said to her female friend, gold dripping down her neck. A month later, the chains were gone, and she and her girlfriend were thirsty.

"Hey Magic, you got anything?" she asked.

"Here, you and your girlfriend split this." I gave her a dime piece. I emphasized saying "split it" because I wanted them to fight. I watched them squabble for crumbs, saying to myself I never get that bad, but something I hadn't learned was that I couldn't see my ears. This life that I chose didn't permit me to see the pain in others; their pain and suffering had nothing to do with me or my family, and I knew that.

September 28, Saturday morning, was the day of my mother's birthday party. My sisters told me to make sure I got there for the party. Funny, they think it was only their mother, being I haven't lived with my mother for many years. I still remember the hard times we went through trying to keep a roof over our heads, struggling for food, all sleeping in one bed; when one peed, we all got wet. Well, none of them know or remember the cold winters with no heat or hot water.

On a beautiful moonlit Saturday night, Seneca and Crissy were at the track on Hunts Point. We were a regular out there on Seneca and Garrison Avenue, so I didn't have to go out there with them all the time. They knew the routine and the expected amount; the two of them, good for a hundred an hour or more. It'd been three hours already, so I was thinking about showing up at my mom's birthday party. I knew she knew I was a pimp by now; all knew I kept rock and money. I know they were waiting for me to get this party started. I was also ready to go as soon as my hoes came back with this dough.

Before that could happen, my brother rolled up in his Monte Carlo. He said, "Brother. Get in. Mommy had a stroke. I come to get you."

"What? A stroke?" I was numb, and all got quiet in my head until he pulled me, "Say, come on."

"No, you go, I come later. I gotta wait till my hoes come back from the track."

"What? Your mom's had a stroke and may be dying, and you got to wait for some bitches!! Are you for real?"

"I will meet you there, my brother." I definitely needed a hit now and a drink while I waited for my money from the point. It wasn't long before they came back, and I was on my way. Got there around one o'clock; they were still partying.

"Oh, no, all these people here, I don't know. Get the fuck out right now!" I said.

"No, Jimmy. Mommy wanted this party," my sisters said.

"Well, somebody, tell me what happened, and if I don't know you, only family and close friends, the rest get the fuck out. She ain't want this party bad enough to have a stroke, these nosey-ass people, get it, get the fuck moving."

All the ranting and raving was for nothing. My mother was brain-dead and had been on life support for two days. My uncle and brother made the final word, taking her off.

Oh, the hurt I felt could only be numbed with a constant flow of drugs, alcohol, and sex every day and night! Jack Daniels, Jim Beam, wild turkey, freebasing 'til the time of the funeral. I barely made it to that. I had to be helped in and out. There can be no greater pain in the world to me right now. With the help of friends and family, we were able to get a four-plot gravesite for the first Holloway, who went way too soon. And if I don't get myself together soon, I'll be next.

Sleeping in crack houses and hotels with different women, I caught jaundice; my eyes and skin were yellow, pissing Coca-Cola. Dick raw from women sucking it and me stretching it and pulling it, trying to get it inside the pussy when it's soft and can't get hard. I guess at that time, the little head had more sense than I had. It was not going to get hard. And I was glad that a nut wasn't what I needed. AIDS was being talked about more now.

I was smoking like a mad Russian. If you want to smoke with me, shit, gotta do something. They say it won't get hard.

Well, keep licking till it does while I take this hit. Less talking, more sucking. Give me a big blast like you, and then I will blow some smoke on it, Magic.

All the time I'm waiting for you to do it, she's running her mouth. I spent a hundred dollars before I found out the bitch couldn't suck dick. Living foul, sometimes not bathing for days, always thinking about the next one. It got worse for my girl; she was disappearing for weeks at times, but I didn't care. I was fighting a demon, and they were winning. I couldn't let it claim both of us.

Sometimes, when we were together, I watched her while she was sleeping. She shook and moaned as if tormented. I thought to myself that this was not what I wanted. The money we made was being used to destroy our lives. My mother was 47; I believe drugs played a big part in her death. Drugs, money, ill-gotten, will do you no good.

I was straddling the fence of good and evil. The way my life was going, I would have to kill someone, or someone was going to kill me. I had to make a choice about who I was going to serve.

# Chapter Six
## Deepest Greetings to All up There

Living a drug-filled life was taking a toll on me and all that I loved. Parts of me were dying. I sold some dummies at a known drug spot in Harlem for a quick hundred and ran back to the Bronx to cop. This particular time, I went back a second time, thinking enough time had passed for the ones I picked to be gone. Once arriving, I saw Vick was gone.

No, they must have been waiting, for I was surrounded with a pistol to my head.

"Is this him?"

"Yeah!!"

At that moment, I felt a punch to the side of my head, stunning me briefly and removing all light. The sounds I heard and felt were a weapon to my head, and the words, "I should shoot you," the voice said.

Then, there was another voice. It was Cynthia Brown, my old childhood friend who was driving Silver Shadow when I hit this quick lick. They must have seen the car make a U-turn. She called out, "Jimmy!!"

I broke for the car. While running, the one I picked caught up and hit me in the face with a bottle, gashing it as it exploded on my face. Feeling blood flowing down my chest, I dove into the car without opening the door.

"Drive!!"

My face was a mess. We headed over the bridge to Lincoln Hospital. After they stitched me up, I laid low at Cynthia Brown's place while I recovered. It was right off Boston Rd. I stayed in the basement for a short time.

I didn't take to church and God so much as a child, and not having a father, it was difficult to love a man, specifically a white one. The picture I saw in the Bible that my grandmother had scared me. I couldn't identify, not my people. Yet, I knew I needed a greater strength. Mine had been weakened. This was the second time. Clearly, the benefits of pippin hoes while supporting a drug habit were dangerous. Next time, I might not be so lucky. Let's reset.

After a couple of days' rest, I was back out smoking. Seneca was horrified when she first saw me like I was a god that couldn't be hurt. It seemed she was more hurt than I was. I assured her I was okay.

She smiled, "You're still handsome."

"Well, I've been thinking, baby, this game is rough. You and I need a break, a fresh start, a new approach. I'm enrolling in school for nursing. You go in the afternoon, and I come in the evening while you're leaving. Give this lifestyle a break. It will be here."

Well, our intentions were good, but we didn't tell our drug habits what we planned. Now, while both of us were going to school, our money was low. We tried our best. We weren't like other drug heads; I needed a G or better. With that, I didn't want big money, but still, money was needed, not for no runs.

Things were looking bright. It was so good seeing her at school when I came in as she was leaving. Three weeks ago, one day, I came to school looking to see her. Her teacher said she didn't come in today. My heart fell to my stomach. It was so hard to complete class or think of anything else, only what happened and where she could be.

Being a Scorpio and she a Pisces, we, well, I had an uncanny ability to sense or predict where she'd be or go. I knew she was still using it; the question was, when I found out, what was I going to do? Was I going to use it too?

It was good and dark when I got up to the Bronx on Park and Washington One-Hundred-Sixty-Seventh Street, right by the post office. I was thinking about what I was going to say to her about using. Here she comes with that sexy walk and big, beautiful smile, happy to see me. I was also glad.

"Come on, Daddy," she said.

"Wait, where are you going?"

"To Nicey's house. Come, I've got three twenties."

"Then what are we gonna do after that?" I asked.

"I'm going home," she said.

Three twenties would only get me started, and I knew that, and that greedy bitch Nicey. Just as I was thinking no, someone gets out of a car to mail a letter and drops a hundred-dollar bill. While I'm thinking that sixty is not enough, the hundred-dollar bill is waving in the wind and darkness is shining. Gift? But from who? It's Magic.

The beasts were unleashed till things were back to normal if smoking every day is normal. I stayed in school, got the certificate, and even did some internship at St. Luke's Hospital. Seneca stopped going. We were able to put four or five days together before the gnawing in my stomach with a pocket full of money, getting ready to shit before I got the crack would hit. Yeah, I got the certification but was not ready to use it. I remember going to cop in my white uniform.

Seneca was still out there, and I wasn't leaving her. Being that I turned her on to this life, I am responsible, though I didn't start her on crack. I tried all that I knew, which is nothing, on how to stop. Shit, she still looks good; no one could ever guess.

One time, I told her, "Don't bring that crack in this house no more. If you do, it's over." Shit, she still had her job at Paradise Alley and was good for a G or better any night.

This one afternoon, I was starving, thinking about what I was going to eat. The doorbell was ringing rapidly. I opened the door, and Seneca was standing there with two D'Agostino shopping bags. The first thing she said was, "I guess I won't be seeing you anymore," as she gave me the two bags.

"I got to go to the bathroom," she said and went. I took the two bags to the kitchen; they were all kinds of goodies. I had paid no mind to what she had said. As I put things away, I noticed she was taking a long time in the bathroom. I went there to open the door; she was sitting on the bowl with the smoking stem in hand, slowly releasing smoke from her nose and mouth.

I reached for and grabbed the stem. She held tight. I pulled. "Let go," I said.

"I'm not holding it; it's holding me," she said.

"You got more of that?"

"Yeah, here." She gave me a fresh pack, two missing.

"And how much money you got?"

"About eight hundred, and I brought the food and the cab from downtown."

"Give me," I said as I counted it. My dick started to get hard when she talked that submissive baby talk, "Anything you want, Daddy."

Shit, I had loaded up her stem and had my dick out. The bathroom reminded me of Billie and Diana Ross in *Lady Sings the Blues*. Only I'm with it for the moment. I'm not throwing shit away.

"Right now, baby, suck my dick while I take this hit." As I pulled a nice long poke with my dick in her mouth, things weren't that bad.

I was interested in the letter P. as a young boy pertaining to my life and work and occupation: players, pimps, pushers, physicians, priests, prophets, and politicians. I felt I had completed three. Prostitution money was slow with the AIDS virus and crackheads sucking dick for five dollars or a hit.

We were way above that low money—once-a-week or once-a-month crackheads. And the women knew I was getting it good. But you have to suck some dick good, and when I say, don't be shy when I want someone else to suck this dick.

And if she does it better than you? You're outta here. I don't have money or time to waste. Because when the money or crack runs out, the whole illusion and fantasy stop. If you're trying to get your little shrunken crack dick sucked with no drugs or money, you really feel like a damn fool. You just had eight hundred dollars. You were the man. Now if it costs you a nickel to shit, you have to throw up.

Two days running from spot to spot, who got the best hotels. Clubs would get boring if I couldn't light up. Then came the time that Seneca didn't come home from work. The whole night into morning, I searched all the spots, me and Silver Shadow, five spots in the Bronx. Shit, I was determined to find her. Tired, I fell asleep, beginning a new search tomorrow.

Tomorrow came quickly, the sun licking me. I heard a knock on the door and someone saying, "Open the door, it's me."

"Seneca!" I jumped up to open the door to her beautiful face and smile. I was so glad to see her, as she was to see me.

"Give me a stem, baby. I need a hit bad right now!"

"What happened?" I asked.

"I was coming home in a cab, and I took a hit in the back seat. The next thing, as we were driving, a cop pulled us over. The driver told the police that I had smoked some drugs back there. They searched me, found the bundle, and took me to jail. I'm just getting out. That's all I got for the five minutes. But what the judge said changed our lives completely."

Well, the police didn't take her money like they did mine. They didn't even find drugs on me but took my money anyway. The judge told her that since it was her first offense, she would suspend the sentence for two years if she went and completed an in-house program for a year. She wipes clean her charges!

Wow, this was good news to me. I had a way out, even though I would miss her and the money. I was battling a hard addiction myself and needed help. I told her that I wanted to stop, too. Before the week she had to go, we got so high and freaked out. I brought a fifth of Wild Turkey and took it into the bedroom, where I licked and stuck every hole, plowing that butt hole while cursing and swigging bourbon, smacking that ass. It would be the last time.

The week went by fast, and it was time for her to leave. On the way downtown to Port Authority for the bus trip to rehab, she asked, "Baby, what are you going to do when I leave?"

"Chill, baby. I'm done with this life," I replied.

"What are you going to do with all my outfits?" she asked.

"I'm going to throw them away, baby." And she had a lot of them: wigs, high heels, baby dolls, lingerie.

"You sure?"

"Yes, baby, I'm done."

"Well, here baby, I saved a little money up," she said, then she gave me fifteen hundred dollars.

"What, you been holding out?"

"No, my steady knew I was leaving and gave me two thousand."

"You're the best baby ever; be a girl as wonderful as you. Six months will go by fast. I'll be clean when you come back. Call me as soon as you can. Bye, baby."

She got on the bus, and we waved goodbye. The lights and sounds of Times Square went out. I couldn't hear or see anything. My baby was gone, and nobody could ever replace her. No time to feel sad; it's a good thing for her. Now, I've got to work on myself.

I asked God to take my life off this planet if I use it again, and I meant it. Be careful what you ask for because God has a funny way of giving you what you ask for. With that, I headed back uptown to the club, thinking about how I was going to put this fifteen hundred to work. I wouldn't be getting another lump sum like this for a while. But I'm still Magic, and I've got a plan.

Well, now she's gone, and I'm sort of on my own. Without a woman, I had gotten tired of pimping hoes. After seeing the inside of this game and its price for a temporary high and pleasure, treading through the darkness looking for pleasures that only Satan can offer, I've been straddling the fence long enough to know how deadly these pleasure-seeking desires will leave you. Empty and devoid of spirit. If you sell your soul for a dollar, you can't buy it back for a trillion.

Well, it's been a month now since she's gone, and I've been clean. I guess with the prayers and determination, I moved in another direction, taking that money and my fresh, clean attitude. Coot, an old country boy who threw me the stick that day when the boy's father gave him a baseball bat, yeah, we will always be close friends. Our families are always looking out for one another.

Well, we leased a club with some negotiations and some cash. We were now owners of a club, following right along with plan B. Excited I was, we sat down together and came up with a name. Trying to keep within the regulations of having a private sports club, we named it Saltwater's Club. We remodeled the whole place. Coot was a master carpenter, so his skills in that department were far beyond excellent. Then we had smooth and always cool DJ Doug, who knew how to cater to a mature crowd. I was great in promotions. Although it was called Saltwater's, it was really Club Magic.

Soon, we were ready to open with a slightly raised floor to create a dance floor, with tables and chairs behind a rail. The grand opening was delayed by a tragic club fire at Happy Land on Southern Blvd. We had to change the ways the doors opened, and a lot of police made unwanted appearances. We complied completely, and the grand opening was set. The purchase of liquor, beer, and wine, hiring barmaids, and distributing flyers all was going great. I was nervous. I hadn't used it for a month and some change, and I hadn't spoken to my girl in the drug program. I wanted to surprise her with my transformation while she was away. That and the club kept me focused.

Oh, man, this night was on fire. Everybody was showing up, the vibes were good, and we quickly sold out almost everything! All the regulars were dressed up. Knuckles and his drug crew, Tyrone, and Don—we had all grown up together.

They worked for someone; I didn't, plus I was getting more money than they were, so I guess they were a little jealous of the women that I had. When they tried flashing their bankrolls, it was only re-up money. I told them to pull out a gee and said, "Like this every day, money to burn."

Knuckles actually checked me every day to see if I had a gee on me. Sometimes I didn't have it, but they thought I did.

Then there was Israel and his father, Big Bill, who was the landlord of the club we rented. Big respect for his father and Uncle Tee, two old-time bank robbers I heard. Israel was spoiled, disrespectful, and arrogant, given everything by his father, who was very respectful.

When his father wanted him to do anything, he didn't have time. Once, I heard Big Bill curse him, saying, "You ain't worth shit, I should have shot you in the toilet bowl." College-educated, he was about picking up junk and abandoned cars in his flatbed truck.

We ran them out to New Jersey for some quick cash, then went roller skating at Harlem Rooftop or Roxy downtown.

That's one thing he did better than me—skate. He had some style. Nothing like grooving around the rink high on cocaine, sailing to the music. Oh, and chess, he was good at that, too. Well, he could beat me. I knew nothing about it, but shooting pool and basketball, I tore his ass out of the frame. We were very competitive. The only thing he could beat me in was chess. He wanted to play that all the time so he could gloat and brag about whipping me in something. My knuckle game was tight, a known fact. We never took it there.

But there was his brother, doing time up north, who I never met. He was due to be released or paroled. The neighborhood was excited. He was no joke, but fear or respect wasn't my concern. Rent was paid to Big Bill, his father, so there should be no problems.

Man, I miss my girl. Days were like weeks. I still kept a roll and was making money at the club. This one weekend, from what I'd saved and made, was well over fifteen hundred dollars. Forgetting how far I'd come and void of praise, I used big time. Revisiting all the old spots and the same habits and pleasures, I went to Connie's. She always keeps a few hoes and drug dealers in her house. She does heroin and smokes crack. A beautiful, tall, fat-ass girl, she stays hustling and getting high.

If there wasn't a girl there capable of sucking a good dick, she goes out and gets one. Usually, there's more than one there at any given time. They give you the nod that they're ready and willing to do whatever it takes to please you without saying a word.

Once that's established, I give Connie the money for the room and money to get more drugs and her things. Every time I ask her to get me one also, she never brings one back. If she did, she tapped the shit out of it, so I barely got a chance to chase the dragon, which was a good thing, I guess.

In her own way, she cared about me and didn't want me to get hooked.

After a two-day run, I was broke and disgusted. I sat on the steps in the morning hours, around ten, contemplating my next move. The girl Angie walked by. I'd seen her, but my mind was on something else. She had fallen off greatly from selling to use. A few months ago, me and Silver Shadow were cruising on Park Ave. I saw her and a few girls walking, looking thirsty.

"What up!!" Angie turned and came over to the car.

"What's up with that Spanish girl? Does she get high?"

"It's my birthday," she said. "Give me a hit."

"Yeah, OK, but I want to get with that Spanish girl. Where y'all going?"

"Project 748, Apt. 8E."

"OK, let me park. I'll meet you there."

Once inside, I paid for privacy, then tried to get that Spanish girl in the room. Instead, Angie kept pestering me about it being her birthday, asking for another hit, and letting me know she was willing to do whatever. Not interested, I kept telling her, but she was persistent. Finally, I let her suck my dick, which she was begging to do. She did it for at least three seconds, then asked for the fourth hit. I did my best to get out of there. I was gone with none of the eight I had in the beginning. Happy birthday!

I continued to use it for the rest of the night until early morning. While exhausted and broke, sitting on the steps, completing my next steps, I saw Angie walk by. So, you see, even in my drug haze, it was still clear I didn't really want to speak to her. After she passed, I said to myself, "Go on up to grandma's and get some rest. You can't undo what's been done."

Busted and disgusted, with the stim still in my pocket, I started walking up the hill toward Boston Road. No more than ten minutes after seeing her, while walking up the hill, police sirens were heading right towards me.

"Hands out of your pockets, up against the wall. You're under arrest for rape!!"

"What, what! Rape? You have the wrong one."

"Well, hold still. The victim is on her way to identify you."

I felt good about that, for I never had a problem getting pussy. Less than a minute later, another car pulled up. A cop asked me to turn around. As I did, I saw Angie in the back seat. I can't remember if I said it out loud or to myself, "That's Angie. She'll tell you." That's when the handcuffs came out, and he started reading me my rights.

This is unbelievable. Although I was still in a drug state of mind, the police threw my stim away, saying, "This charge of rape is what you need to worry about." With that said, I was thrust into the back seat en route to the 42nd precinct, where I could make a call. I'll be out in a couple of hours.

Man, was I wrong. After hours at the precinct, I was taken to central booking to see the judge.

Judge: "You, Mr. Holloway, have been charged with the crime of rape and sodomy. How do you plead?"

"Not guilty, your honor," my court-appointed lawyer said.

Judge: "This case shall come before me a month from now."

"Excuse me, your Honor, I'll be on vacation that month. Can we make it sometime next month, giving me time to prepare?"

"OK, the following month, September second. Nine thirty a.m. Bail will be set at two hundred thousand. Case adjourned."

What just happened? Rape? Sodomy? Is this a dream? Let me go back to sleep, deep sleep, to wake up with a better wake-up and figure out why and how I got here and how I was going to get out.

"Holloway, Jimmy J. Holloway," the guards said again, waking me up from a deep sleep.

"Let's go, you're being transferred to Rikers Island."

This is real.

I guess it was sometime after dark when I got on the bus, looking out the window at the people walking free, mostly going home. I was going home, too, at least for the next couple of months or less. I was still hoping to get in touch with someone who would talk with Angie getting her to realize her mistake. I'll make some calls to the island.

On the way, I met someone bigger than I was, sort of schooling me on what to expect upon arriving. The young boys were going cray-cray up in there. While in the reception area, getting our sheets and pillows, he was digging up in the ceiling, looking for a piece of metal to fashion a weapon out of. He found a three-inch piece of metal, looked at it, and then threw it on the floor, saying it was too small. After listening to his story on how rough it was inside, I picked it up. Shit, I could make something out of it. At that moment, a voice inside said, "Trust me, I got you. I know your fear; no harm will come to you." With that, I threw the small piece of metal away.

So, with showering and bedding issued, I was on my way to the pod. Walking down a long corridor towards my pod, being heckled by the other inmates who could tell we were new, I heard, "Yo bitch, y'all smell like pussy." Then I heard a voice calling, "Jimmy, what up? You come to my house?" I turned and looked. It was Terry from around the way, the one who was always trying to sell crap to get the next one. I used to tell him to throw away that crap, then give him a hit or two.

Now, Terry had just come from up top doing a two-to-five. He was diesel, and his face had a new glow, too. "Jimmy, man, good to see you. Yo, this is my man Magic from around the way. Boogie Down in the house. Yo, Magic, take that bed by the window. You need soap, cigarettes? I got you."

He sure helped to take the edge off and brought me into the house like a G, and that had a calming effect on me. I still had a lot to learn about this game. I slept well that night.

The morning came quickly. I was awoken by a strange sound that I had never heard before, "Allahu Akbar, Allahu Akbar," early before the sun was up. Strange, I thought. Soon, the sun was up, and it was time to go to breakfast. Terry taught me how to sit with one leg out from the table in case trouble came. I wouldn't be confined. It was a madhouse coming and going, the air filled with tension, so many inmates.

Terry pointed out Mother, a homo gangster, six-five, three hundred pounds, who liked to give out Twinkies and put them on your bed when he wanted to sexually assault you. "Whatever you do, if it happens to you, don't eat the Twinkie," we laughed.

The time went by quickly. Less than a week before court, there was limited drama in the pod if you followed the rules. One rule is when the lights go out, play your bunk. Do not come to the bubble unless it's life and death. There were Spanish inmate monitors that upheld that rule. They were the only ones up, and once or twice, I saw them inside the bubble while the officers had a cocaine or sex party in the back. Maybe freebasing. All I saw was that every time they came back to the bubble, they were sweating and putting on their clothes, male and female. Sometimes, others showed up.

There was one female officer I liked. She was always in the corridor when I went to chow. I started passing her notes when I passed with words like, "I want to hold your head in my hands, look deeply into your eyes, smell the breath from your nostrils as you slowly exhale and sigh. Surrendering unto me the hunger of your soul for the first time." Ah, man! She looked for me and was hungry for the letter. I was reeling her in. If I didn't beat this charge, she might be a way out. Never underestimate the power of the pen.

What my heart was really thinking about was Seneca in drug rehab, how she was doing, and if she was still there. Time passed slowly here in the module. Nothing exciting happened other than the corrections officers' party on the weekends until five days before my court date. Something changed my life.

This afternoon, while watching *In Living Color* in the day room, there was a lot of commotion in the hall coming this way. Screaming and hollering. The bubble command opened the doors, and in burst six guards with one inmate, a tall, light-skinned brother, handcuffed, kicking, and screaming. They brought him into the day room. As soon as they took off the cuffs, this brother started picking up chairs and began bashing the windows, trying to escape. He was bleeding and still cussing uncontrollably.

The guards addressed the goon squad or house gang. "You're going to let this chump tear up y'all day room?" They started gathering, trying to form Voltron. Enough gathered and were ready to attack when someone asked, "Is that brother Muslim?" Another said, "I think so." And they backed up. The brother, totally exhausted, calmed down, but the anger was still in his face.

"Hey brother, would you like some water?"

"Yes, my brother, thanks."

"Magic's my name," I said, extending my hand.

"Mohammed X," he said.

125

"You Muslim?" I asked.

"Yes, my brother. FOI, following the Honorable Minister Louis Farrakhan."

"Oh, yeah, I'm familiar with them. Well, I'm studying to get my X. What was that beef with the guard about?"

"They violated my rights, disrespected the way I pray, and didn't recognize the Fruits of Islam as a religion. We must stand and demand our rights, or they will trample over you."

So, I helped the brother get adjusted, and we talked a lot. Then he was transferred to HDM, a more prison-like upstate facility where you stay in cells. I guess they didn't want any problems with Farrakhan speaking about separation up in here, spoiling their operations.

Anyway, I'm not trying to get involved with none of this shit. I'm minding my business and trying to get out. I've spoken to a few people about what happened, and they all know me and the girl, so I'll be getting out at this court date because there's no evidence. It never happened, and she'll say she made a mistake. I learned my lesson, and I'll get back to the club, which was booming now in full swing. I'll jump back in and take it to the next level.

I don't think I slept the night before.

"Holloway, 1199712. Court."

I looked at the clock. 3:30.

'Allah Akbar,' Allah Akbar. That sound puzzled me every morning after talking to Brother X Muhammed. I found out it was prayers. I needed prayers right about now, and I know they work. This was God answering my prayers when I asked Him to take my life off this planet if I used it again, and jail was that.

The ride to court was incident-free, a bright, beautiful morning. Clearly, the bus missed the turn, bypassing criminal court and pulling up to the Supreme Court. Maybe they were dropping some inmates off and then taking me back to be released. The guard was calling names, and they were stepping out.

"Jimmy Holloway, 1199712. Step out."

"Officer, there might be a mistake. I should be in criminal court."

"You're Jimmy J. Holloway, 1199712?"

"Yes."

"OK, you're in the right place. You've been indicted."

The words sucked all the air out of the unloading dock as the gate came down, and the last bit of light disappeared. How could this be, I thought to myself. My charges weren't ones to share. I would have to wait and see what the court-appointed attorney had to say. I slept with my ears open and eyes closed.

I waited in that cramped, cold, crowded cell with seconds seemingly like hours. The chatter of the other inmates was not as loud as the slow tick of my watch.

"Holloway!!" The guard shouted as I opened my eyes to the reality that I was still in jail. Through a corridor, he led me to a room with a booth and a chair on both sides. I sat in the empty chair, my lawyer on the other across from me, looking at some papers.

"Mr. Holloway, good morning; how are you?"

"I'm in jail! How good is that?"

"Well, I'm looking at your charges. They're pretty severe: rape, sodomy, and sexual assaults. Sexual misconduct carries a penalty of eight to fifteen. The judge set the bail at a hundred thousand. Can you get bail?"

"I can't make a down payment on a frankfurter. Nor can my family or friends. Listen, I've never been in jail, I have no record, and this girl is a crackhead and she's lying. There's no proof."

"Well, they have a rape kit and the victim's testimony."

"Well, my DNA is not on it. I know that."

"Well, I'll see if I can get you released on your own recognizance. Ready?"

Being released on my own recognizance was out of the question, and so was the bail. Because I said I knew her, I might threaten or harm her. Back to the Rock, and I was mad and scared. How long would this go on? Almost two more months before I came again to court, I thought on the ride back, looking through the grated windows on the bus.

All of a sudden, up at the front of the bus, hollering and screaming. Two inmates were stabbing another inmate with an object, and this inmate had a cast on one arm, so he was not handcuffed. The other two were handcuffed together. I cannot tell if they were together, stabbing the other, who was bleeding a lot. Suddenly, the cast guy pulls out his stabber and starts stabbing back. What a shock the other two had when they felt their blood flowing, and he caught both by surprise. They backed up, giving both a chance to lick their wounds.

The driver had put on the siren and floored it up the Cross Bronx Expressway, over the Whitestone Bridge, hitting those slowdown bumps at forty miles an hour, throwing inmates in the back up to the ceiling. When they came smashing down, you could hear the moans and groans. The driver had radioed ahead, saying there was an emergency situation, code blue, and multiple bleeding casualties.

When the bus pulled in, a regiment of correction officers was there, escorting each one separately and, after searching them, asking what they saw. Everyone said nothing. Most said they were sleeping and needed medical attention also. I was in the front, but those in the back were flying up to the ceiling and then crashing down to the seats. I'm sure there were plenty of injuries.

I just wanted to get back to the module. I was tired all day in court hearing the same shit. Another two months before I see the judge.

I wasn't getting any visitors. Maybe some believed I did it, with my lifestyle and being a conceited ass motherfucker. Good for his ass. He thought he was all that. There were always going to be haters. I had to get in contact with the ones who cared and knew me and this girl. But I had nobody's phone number, just their names and addresses. Time to get to writing.

While writing letters, I got in touch with my spiritual side, able to write to my heart's desires. I wrote to my old girlfriend Genice, a childhood friend who knew my heart. Dr. Joseph Edward, like a brother to me, and Coot, who had thrown me the mop stick. They both knew this girl, Angie. Every day, I thought I was going to be released, but that wasn't happening. Fear of being prosecuted for perjury kept her from telling the truth and admitting she lied.

While writing late at night, I got to see the corrections officers carrying on in the bubble. I mean, having a fucking party, music, sex, and drugs, while an inmate looked out. They told me to play my bunk when they saw me looking. Too late; I saw it already.

I was transferred the next day to HDM, a more prison-like jail. They said you stayed in a cell like upstate prisons, still jail. I'll admit, I was a little scared, and I'll miss Officer Wright, who I was sending letters to regularly, and my man Terry from around the way, who brought me in.

Well, God, it's your world. Would you believe my cellmate was Mohammed X, the defiant one who tried to break out the moment they took off the handcuffs? He was glad to see me, as I was him. He was writing to Farrakhan, trying to get accepted into the Fruits of Islam and trying to establish a mosque where FOI. Muslims can pray differently from Ansari or Sunni Muslims. He greeted me, "Assalamu Alaykum." We talked a lot, and I was interested in all Muslim sects, wondering why they didn't get along.

So, being curious and with my newfound ability to write, I got offered a job writing in the Riker's Island Newsweekly. Oh, man, time flies when you're keeping busy. Going to the law library and learning more about my case, the cobwebs were gone. I impressed myself with my ability to write. Plus, no sex. They say your writing intensifies when you're not skeeting your brains out.

It's been six months. Word got to me that the club, Saltwater, was banging. Every week, big crowds, money being spent, champagne flowing. Knuckles, Don, and a few others hooked up with Joe, Israel's brother, and they were hijacking trucks, getting hundreds of dollars to pay. That's right up my alley, driving and getting paid.

While I'm locked up for bullshit…

HDM Shakedowns, shutdowns, lockdowns, cell doors opening and closing, lights out. Here's another time the cell opens late at night, and then there's the noise of a woman having sex with an inmate. OK, some big fish were locked up, and if you had money or power, a lot of things you could get here. Everything but your freedom. That's all I want. So, I read and write to ease my mind. I wasn't scared, just worried that I might lose this case and be sentenced to eight to fifteen years with a charge of rape.

Well, my next-door cellmate was scared. He was short and had a good reason to be scared. He conned me into holding his six-inch metal stabber, saying if I needed it anytime, he would give it to me. Well, it was thick and surely capable of inflicting serious hurt. "You can hold it tonight," he said. "Hide it somewhere."

"OK," I said. I stuck it in between my mattress.

Would you know the next morning was a shakedown? They found the shank. Of course, I said I had never seen it before and didn't know how it got there. Well, they wrote me up, and I'll have to explain it to the judge, meaning that an in-house hearing to explain how I think it got there. That's in two days. I'd probably go to the Bing, solitary confinement.

Shorty next door acted like he was concerned and gave me some of his commissary stamps and envelopes. But I think he knew a shakedown was coming. Well, wouldn't you know, on my way to chow, walking down the corridor, who do I see with captains' bars? A friend I used to play basketball with behind Yankees Stadium.

"Captain Hardy," I said.

"Magic, what are you doing here?"

"I'm innocent," I said. I explained to him my dilemma, and he took my name and said he would be in touch. That felt good; he recognized me as a good man and a hell of a basketball player. He said most of the people I was playing with were correction officers. I didn't care who they were; I was fearless. I came to play. Magic was the perfect name for the player I was. I used to tear their asses up out there. Sure, he remembered me.

But the next morning, I was transferred to the Bing for two months with no commissary. I lost my writing job and the friends I made. Still jail.

Early morning, "Holloway, One-one-nine-nine-seven-one-two, pack your shit. You're being moved, just your clothes, no commissary, only legal documents, and religious articles." Four officers for one inmate. Wow, this is going to be hard, I thought and tried to prepare myself to be by myself. If I ever needed God for comfort and strength, it was now.

It was a small cell with bars all on one level. Even though there were bars, when I stepped in, and they shut the door, all the air seemed to be sucked out, and the loud noise of the metal door closing was frightening. The guard let me know when I was to eat, shower, and exercise in a private yard for two hours, shower, and then back in the cell. After the first week, it got easier. We were able to talk to each other, sing, tell jokes, and we had a lot of time to read and dream. Sleeping was a way of escaping the reality. Books were read and passed around.

Also, there was a lot of masturbating every other night. I didn't need to have pictures; my memories were vivid. I remembered driving under the George Washington Bridge with two girls, feet away from the river, to freebase. I took the sunroof out of the Silver Shadow, standing up through the roof, and the two girls would take a hit. While one was smoking, the other was sucking my dick. Ecstasy.

I had many episodes, enough to fill a hundred or more pages. But that's irrelevant now; I don't remember them. What I do remember is my girl, Seneca, and I haven't heard from her since she went to the program. It's been six months now.

Two weeks here in solitary confinement, reading the Bible, psalms, scriptures memorized, meditating on the word. My pastime was reading Psalm 91, memorizing it word for word every night.

Then, one day, the guard allowed me to clean a cell that an inmate had been transferred from. Sweep and mop? Sure, anything to get out of the cell for a while. They discarded all the stuff and anything I wanted I could keep. What I saw and wanted was a Quran—a little damaged, with multiple pages missing, thrown in the pile of garbage. I couldn't wait to get it back to the cell to begin reading!

I was extremely excited to get back to my cell to begin reading the Quran. It seemed pages had been ripped out. But the mystery of the pages that were there stimulated my interest. With all the time in confinement, I easily ran through it quickly and found a lot of similarities to the Bible. I thought about Muhammed because he has one and could answer my many questions.

What's more important is what's happening in the morning. Court today, and I'm expecting to be released after no evidence, no witness. If they do have a rape kit, not my DNA. Shit, it's been seven long months. It's either prepared for trial or dismissed for lack of proof. The lawyer says they're prepared to reduce the charges to sexual misconduct.

"What!! I'm not pleading guilty to Jack Bone Nittily Scone. Not copping out to nothing. That's what you tell them."

In court, would you believe the prosecutor walked by and spoke, "If you cop out to sexual misconduct, you'll be out today."

I didn't even think about that for a second. Is he crazy? Get me back to the island. Don't bring me back here unless we're going to trial. What good are you always on vacation? I'm in solitary confinement. Can you do anything about that? It's been eight months. This is what you have—a cop-out.

I've gotten used to being locked up and wanted to get back. Well, I guess we prepare for trial? Yes, this is not going to be a time served. So tired when I got back; no drama.

Early morning, I awoke to a transfer to the population. "Pack your shit, Holloway. C.95."

Another jail, only a dorm again. This time, nobody greeted me at the door jubilantly, but there was an interesting scene. This house was segregated. The Spanish, the gangster Blacks, and the Muslims. Someone saw the Quran I was carrying and said, "He's Muslim."

Then, two others stepped to me and spoke, "Assalamu alaykum."

"Salamu Alaykum," I greeted them back, and then we embraced.

"What's your name, brother?" he asked.

I said, "Magic." I wanted to say a Muslim name, but I knew not. "Magic's my name. Not trying to let anyone get personal. I'm here on a rape charge. I'm not Muslim," I said, away from anyone.

"We're all Muslims, some just don't know it yet. Welcome, Akee."

Man, C-95 was off the chains. I mean slashing every day, twice on Sundays, in the mess hall, yard, to and from court. Lockdown, headcount, play your bed. But it was so good to get away from solitary confinement. The ratio was gangsters eight, Spanish fourteen, Muslims four, including me. So, wonder why they embraced me, so it's about numbers. The rest were herbs, cattle, and sheep to be preyed upon.

One night, the Spanish were walking around late, snapping their fingers, walking around all the beds at two-thirty in the morning. Singling out an herb, then attacking them with pillowcases filled with boots and soap. If you were asleep, you awoke to hollering screams of pain and laughter, hard to distinguish laughter from crying. I lay there praying and hoping they didn't play that game on me. Being half Spanish, I was treated somewhat with respect, although I spoke no Spanish. I just lay there waiting for the morning.

So, I was embraced as a Muslim. They needed numbers because these jailhouse thugs would try you if you appeared weak. That's the way of the world. There's always been strength in numbers, but I had little trust in others unless I was the leader.

One morning, just before court, I had gotten up early to get some jelly for my peanut butter. The guards gave it to the Spanish inmates, and they distributed it to the rest. It was four-thirty a.m. I'm the third person in line. When it's my turn, there's no jelly. I start to flip. "What do you mean there's no jelly? I saw the guard give it to you."

"Oh, okay, it's like that?" I said, taking four milks and three apples. A couple of Black guys were standing behind me saying, "Yeah, yeah, set it off," as the inmate who was distributing the food walked away to tell Poppy, who was still in bed.

"Yo, Magic, Poppy wants to see you." I walked over to his bunk in the dark.

"Yo, Magic, listen. If you want some jelly, ask me. I'll give you, but when you take like that, it causes problems."

"Poppy, listen. I was stressed out with court and shit. My bad. This is your house. I'm good without jelly, my man. That won't happen again." The other inmates were talking, "Yeah, Magic, let's set it."

"Listen, I came here by myself, and that's how I'll leave! If you want to set it off, do that on your own. I'm good without jelly, my man."

Yeah, getting out of this shit is what I'm about, not trying to fall into this now-I-run-my-shit, my-house mentality. This morning, if they don't release me today, I'll file a motion for a speedy trial and start picking witnesses. Oh, yes, I've been reading a lot on my case and have gotten an understanding of what they were trying to do. Also, I read the Quran and learned a little Arabic. I've been contemplating taking my shahada and becoming Muslim.

My witness, Coot, was there at court, willing to testify on my behalf. Simply to say that he knows both parties, and we have known each other for years, and no one has ever called me Chauncey, quite simple. They denied my witness while bringing the accuser from jail also to testify and verify that I was the one who assaulted her. Shit, her record is longer than mine. Forgery, shoplifting, and possession of drugs. A lengthy criminal record. I had to get another witness. They denied Coot.

Jury selection has started, trial three months from today. Coot told me he no longer had the club, and Big Bill died. His son Joe and his crew kind of leaned on Coot, and with no muscles, Coot let it go. He said my girl Seneca came around looking for me. He gave me a number, and my heart skipped. I was ready to go back to the island now! Back in handcuffs on the bus home, the familiar sights and a lot on my mind while crossing Whitestone Bridge. C-95, my home for nine months.

Now, I needed some phone time, wondering how much trouble this would be. I wouldn't need much time, for when I called, this is what she had to say.

"I'm clean now, and I found the Lord."

"Yes, baby," I said.

"I don't think you understand."

"Yes, baby, I do. It's what I wanted. I'm clean, too."

139

"Well, I'm moving. Wish me well. Try finding Jesus. Goodbye."

I was numb, although clean. I didn't have a coming-to-Jesus moment and was actually mad that she mentioned his name. This white Jesus is trying to take my life. Or was I being led on a different path?

After speaking on the phone, I was introduced to a new Muslim inmate. Humsir was a pretty huge brother.

"Assalamu alaykum, my brother. What's your name?"

"Magic."

"He has not taken his shahada yet," the house Imam chimed in.

The odds that I take my shahada had just changed. I was ready.

Humsir, a martial arts expert, began teaching that and his knowledge of the Quran. This Friday, which is Jumma, I will take my Shahada and become a Muslim. While waiting, I was taught how to pray and recite Suras, which are like scriptures in the Bible, and the Surah al-Fatihah, which is like the Lord's Prayer. I was given a sheet of paper with different Arabic surahs. I was learning quickly. I was making seven prayers a day. I was growing spiritually and religiously in the faith.

In addition to the teaching of Kung Fu from Brother Humsir, others were watching too and were secretly plotting.

The word got out that they were going to make a move on the Muslims because they were getting too strong. We spoke to each other quietly and discreetly while observing the gangsters.

After many months on Rikers Island, I came to know that all jails have their goon squads supported and controlled by corrections. The Gulf War was going on, and there was a lot of misconception and hate towards Muslims. So, the order to strike, hit, maim, and kill probably came from up top.

Me and Humsir were preparing for war, going all out. They approached us, our backs against the wall. Seven of them, four of us. This is going to be fun, I thought, until they pulled out these long-ass swords. This piece of metal that I saw was about a foot long. I wouldn't know if and where it was sharp, and I didn't care to find out.

Remembering what my momma had said, "Don't let them hit you with that baseball bat, Jimmy." It was a very tense moment as our Imam spoke with their leader, finding out these chumps were getting worried about our numbers growing and thought we wanted to take over the phone.

"Oh, no, we're not trying to take over anything; we don't need slot time. Only when important, we come to you, Gangster man." And that was that.

I attended Juma on Friday, took my shahada, and became Abdul Jihad Ala Min. I recalled studying the Quran, reciting Arabic, and making prayers seven times a day. I'm wearing a kufi now, walking, and feeling a little different about myself. This week coming is Ramadan, a month of prayer and fasting, giving praise and sacrifice to Allah. All the studying and praying were taking me in a new direction, a way of easing my mind. I was still having drug dreams, getting my dick sucked while taking a hit. Time will tell. It is easy to be clean when in a controlled environment, when on the outside, that's the test.

This Islam stuff was lacking in my gospel music. The music my grandma played while she talked to me and prayed for me with oils and potions in my tub. The trial was soon approaching, and I was praying for my release. Captain Hardy had heard about the beef that occurred and transferred me to Bronx House with a job that pays Suicide Watch. Plus, it was closer to my family and friends, which wasn't much. Bronx House of Detention, another dorm. Still jail.

Now, all this praying and fasting and being innocent of the crime should get me off with a good witness to testify. It was God that had gotten me in; it would be God that would get me out. I was seasoned now to jail. At BHD, there was no outside yard, only a rooftop. Through my windows, I could see the hookers outside plying their wares throughout the night. When one was spotted doing or showing the nasty, we would all run to the windows and watch. Kicking my shit when I saw the orange glow of the flame and the cloud of smoke exhaling, and I'd be lying if I said that didn't bother me. But I couldn't show it. My name, Abdul Jihad Ala Min.

Well, they denied my first witness, Coot, a longtime friend. Why? I don't know. What's left is a stronger witness, Dr. Joseph Edwards. There was a lot of talk going around the block. Some believed I did it and were like, "Good for his ass. He thought he was all that!"

Having a lot of friends, few will know your heart. But Joe and I go way back to before he was a doctor. Eating mackerel and rice, living together through college, and he was like my big brother. I owe a lot to him for my brilliance. I read and listened as he prepared his thesis, reading his book while I stayed there. His roommate was Curtis Vanlierop, also brilliant. Nobody has to lie; just tell the truth. Maybe time off the job was the only cost.

Meanwhile, back at BHD, there was no Masjid, so I wasn't praying anymore but was still wearing my kufi and greeted as such. The phone was easily accessed. Everyone was getting paid suicide pay for checking on the prisoners and selling cigarettes, weed, and dope to all coming in on the visit.

Once, I worked in receiving and saw Slick Rick come through. The young boys had him kicking a rhyme all the time while they were plotting to take the gold out of his mouth. My man Stokes from around the way was there. He said Guy Fisher was down at the tombs and asked him to transfer here. He said no because he had a plan to break out. Security was slack. So, he swept his way right out the door. Nice.

I planned to walk out the door. No felonies or criminal convictions. Yet, I was scared of spending eight to ten years behind bars, being totally innocent. Yes, I was more than worried.

The time I've spent in jail gave me time to reflect on life, trying to pinpoint where it started to go wrong. Was it growing up without a father? Reading those pimp books and watching them in movies, hum! I was a good guy at heart, but some called me conceited. No, I'm just particular about who I associate with! Those incidents that happened when I was a boy left me skeptical but not bitter, just particular about who I relate to or not at all. Did all my stealing, lying, and arrogance growing up hungry lead me here to condemn me now? Some might know of the bad things I did, but only God knows why.

Well, before the trial was to start, after fourteen months, they reduced my bail to five hundred dollars. Yes! That's an amount I could attain. Still, it was not easy when some think you're guilty.

My childhood girlfriend, who I loved at eleven, was my first love. We didn't know anything about love or making it, but kissing I knew well and was good at it. I learned how to bite a little and suck on the tongue while deeply inhaling, taking all the air from their lungs, leaving them spinning. She had my heart early and was still there. She could have paid for it all but thought my brother should contribute also, and he did.

So, after fourteen months of being locked up, I'll be released in the morning. I couldn't sleep last night. The trial was still four months away, but being free will make it easier to fight the case on the outside than inside.

In the morning, going through the process of signing out and picking up my cash and paperwork, getting my pictures and writings of Islam, would you believe my stomach started churning, rumbling, and farting? The thought of taking a hit while getting my dick sucked was heavy on my mind. All that I had learned went out the window.

As soon as the gates opened, my mind was on automatic. With several hundred in my pocket, I knew what I wanted to do. My girlfriend, Genice, was waiting outside the gate, looking beautiful. The air was sweet as the sun-brushed my face. Oh, it was good to be free.

I grabbed Genice and gave her a big hug.

"You want to go to a hotel?" she asked.

"Now, I want to go see my family first, put my bags down. Baby, I'll call you later. Drop me off at my grandma's house. I'll let you know about the hotel."

"Bokie!" Oh, how I missed hearing her call my name. In glee and with tears in her eyes, "You want a jailhouse?" she asked as she pulled the pack of Pall Malls out of her homemade apron where she keeps the scissors. Oh, it was so good to hear my grandma's voice and see the love in her eyes. But I couldn't stay. The strange vibe I felt from the people was cold, and I could feel the eyes and I heard the whispers.

The club Salt Waters was gone, and a lot of people were locked up or being investigated due to Joe and Israel supposedly hijacking trucks, a federal crime. God locked me up in time. I would've gotten some of that money! Here I am, out on bail with a drug habit, and I had no idea how to stop.

So, in the morning, I called Genice, and we headed downtown to book a weekly hotel room close to work. We decided on West Fourteenth Street and Twelfth Ave, New York City. It was away from the drug life in the Bronx. Time to make some money and prepare for my court date, staying out of any and all trouble while out on bail. I didn't feel right up around the people I thought I knew. This was a horrible change.

The teachings of Islam and the Bible helped to change my morals, yet I couldn't commit to either. One thing I knew, I loved gospel music, and Islam wasn't giving me the things I loved. Songs and music saved my soul. Business was good, and I was wondering if a hustler at heart selling bootleg items in Midtown would be very profitable.

Magic had the gift of gab, selling Calvin Klein socks, Kenneth Cole pocketbooks, Donna Karan, Coach, and Prada. Back at the hotel at night, it was transformed into a hub for hookers, drugs, and a way of life. I was making pretty good money at the time, and the night was exciting. Still, it wasn't long before I got involved back in the same old thing. Nights at the Chelsea Hotel were hot in the streets, and I was very familiar with that life.

Hotels like Crosstown Hotel, The Belvedere Hotel on Seventy-Seventh Street, West Side of Broadway—I barely slept in any of them. By the time I wanted to sleep, it was time to check out, and I would rent the room again. At the Belvedere Hotel, I met a white boy who played college football and drank a lot of beer. We became friends because I also played for my school, so we had that in common. He had a girlfriend who was rich. When he went to meet her, her dad pointed to the chandelier and said, "You'd never have that much money at one time in your life." Then he popped a beer, another beer, and another beer.

Now, I don't really drink beer, so when there was no more beer, he wanted me to go out with him to get more beer. I was so drunk I could barely walk. Then I had to go take a piss. I turned around and could not find him; he had disappeared into a white crowd. Shit! They all looked like him, and I couldn't find him. So, I went back to my room. I barely made it without wetting myself.

At Crosstown Hotel on One Hundred Forty-Fifth Street, I'd sometimes rent two rooms: one for me and my girl and one for private prospects and interviews to further my bottom line. Plus, Copeland's Restaurant was right up the block with a delicious breakfast of salmon cakes, grits, and eggs. Genice rented a room in the Chelsea Hotel on the West Side and paid for a week so I could work with her every day in Midtown.

It was not long before a hooker remembered me from Paradise Theater. She was using, and I was using right along with her. She knew all the connections down in that area.

I started using it right along with her. She liked smoking on her knees on the floor, butt-ass naked, and I'd chase her around trying to put my dick in her ass. I was caught up in the drug life again—the sex and fantasy of drug use. I was worried because I was still out on bail, and my court date was coming up. The court dates are far apart, and they are hoping you fuck up in between that time. However, my court date was tomorrow.

The drug dealers I coped with gave me a proposition.

"What is it?" I asked.

"Magic, we got this guy, and we are spending his credit card, so we have to hold him here with you until the morning.

As long as he smokes, you'll smoke, and here is something for you if you agree."

Shit! My hooker friend and I were low on product. It sounded like a good deal.

I said, "Cool! But I have to go to court in the morning. Y'all must be out then."

"Sure, Magic, sure, we have to be gone in the morning."

I made that stupid motherfucker stay in the bathroom to do his shit. Morning came quickly, and they raped his credit cards—TVs, camcorders, and jewelry—and they were not finished in the morning.

"Yo man, I got to go to court. Y'all not finished yet?"

"Magic, we need a little more time. Go ahead to court. We will hit you off. Go ahead to court, and your things will be alright."

What choice did I have? Well, I went to court, and it was adjourned for three more months. Motherfuckers on vacation. That's that trap-off shit! I head back to my room and open the door, and these motherfuckers have shotgun shells open and are putting them into pipes. The bomb construction in my hotel shook me.

I was given bail for six months. It was a trap to give me enough room to hang myself. I couldn't go back home; it didn't feel right anymore. Some, I guess, thought I was guilty. The arrogant ass motherfucker with the AK-47, .357, a shoulder holster, and side clips was over now. I never wanted to see jail again. I thought, if this woman could lie to me for whatever reason and have me locked up for seventeen months in the same neighborhood where we grew up, there's no way of knowing what kind of lies she spread about me to people who are supposed to know me.

I did not want to go back; I'd rather go anywhere but where I grew up. I had six months until the trial resumed, so I started wandering about shelters and checking on ways how I could change my life! I even thought about leaving the country. I did not want to run; I really was innocent.

I went back to my room. No need to explain to me what was going on. Me being an army veteran, these cock suckers are making pipe bombs.

"If y'all don't get that shit outta here right now, you're out of your fucking mind. I just came from the court. If they catch that shit here with me, my ass is cooked. Get to packing that shit up. Rapido."

They weren't moving fast enough for me.

### SO, I PACKED MY SHIT AND LEFT!

What happens next?

Do I change?

Can I Change?

www.ingramcontent.com/pod-product-compliance
Lightning Source LLC
Chambersburg PA
CBHW051203120626
46547CB00012B/1177